A WAY OF PEACE

LENTEN MISSION JOURNAL

Cyclical Calendar
& Curriculum for 2020

guided by The Spiritual Exercises of
André duBignon Furin

Publisher's Cataloging-in-Publication data

LIBRARY of CONGRESS CONTROL NUMBER

Furin, André duBignon

ISBN-13: 978-0-9960554-8-2

Filament Eleven Press
Design and Layout by Dot Dodd

PRINTED IN THE UNITED STATES OF AMERICA

First Paperback February 2020
12 11 10 9 8 7 6 5 4 3 2 1

dedicated to Dr. Jamie Faser Arthur
Teacher, inspirational leader, disciple, and friend

I am tremendously and deeply grateful for Jamie's decades of leadership throughout Catholic education and the Catholic community. I am uplifted and guided by the tangible manifestations of her faith and the way she has deepened it through her practice of a Sacramental life. Dr. Arthur's continued presence in the lay Catholic life gives me great hope for trusting in the Way.

The first edition of this book would not have come to light without her work in encouraging the enthusiastic spirit of our Catholic youth, and, therefore, helping make the best of dreams come true.

A WAY OF PEACE
LENTEN MISSION JOURNAL
Cyclical Calendar & Curriculum for 2020

guided by The Spiritual Exercises of

André duBignon Furin

FOCUS: The Moral Teachings of Jesus with particular emphasis on God's Love within our humanity.

a 96-day curriculum

Ahead-of-time, prepare to take "off" (at least, partial days of retreat with ample "unscheduled" time) Ash Wednesday, [Leap Day,] Sundays, and, especially, Good Friday!

Discover:

What the Life (and Teachings) of Jesus may be all about.

Through:

daily prayers, daily exercises, "extrospection" (experience-through-action), mindfulness meditation, and a path of forgiveness and reconciliation.

Audience:

Those having completed their 1st Reconciliation and 1st Eucharist (i.e. this little book would be a great gift for maturing 2nd graders) -or- for highschool students (i.e. Confirmed Adult Catholics) -and- beyond!

Live a life of:

40 days without judgment (i.e. Luke 6:37-38)
40 days to honor that which is most <u>sacred</u> to each of us about <u>Life</u>!
40 days of Loving-Kindness
40 days of Prayer & Meditation

Purifying our thoughts and actions.

Choose a set of 9 days to pray a Novena (nine successive days of devotional prayer). Mark these 9 days on your calendar and/or highlight them in this journal.

Pray the full cycle of the Mysteries with your rosary in keeping to your requests and intention.

Suggested contemplations for additional inspiration for your Lenten Mission and insight into the moral teachings and God's Love within our Humanity can be found in the "End Notes."

i.e. for the "lighter days" such as Monday, Tuesday, Wednesday, Thursday, and Saturday

Pray aloud each day (optionally) in English (most native familiar vernacular tongue), French (a European tongue), Latin (an ancient tongue), and other (i.e.Egyptian Arabic/ Coptic, a modern-day other-wordly tongue).

Suggested prayers:

Morning Offering (prayers of gratitude and openness, i.e the prayer of Thomas Merton)
Memorare
Nicene Creed
Our Father
Hail Mary

Glory Be (Doxology)
Act of Contrition
Blessings and Thanksgivings before each meal
Evening Offering (prayers of Thanksgiving and adoration)

In regards to "Prayer & Meditation" (adapted from usccb.org in re "prayers and devotions") Forms of prayer may include: blessing; adoration; petition; intercession; thanksgiving; and praise.

"Meditation is above all a quest. The mind seeks to understand the *why* and *how* of the Spiritual / Catholic life, in order to [align and] respond to what the [Holy Spirit] is asking." By meditating on the Gospels, holy icons, liturgical texts, spiritual writings, or "the great book of creation," we come to make our own that which is God's. "To the extent that we are humble and faithful, we discover in meditation the movements that stir the heart and we are able to discern them. It is a question of acting truthfully in order to come into the light: "Lord, what do you want me to do?" (CCC 2705-2706).

Meditation is an essential form of Christian prayer, especially for those who are seeking to answer the vocational question, "Lord, what do you want me to do?"

Spiritual reading of Sacred Scripture, especially the Gospels, is an important form of meditation. This spiritual reading is traditionally called *lectio divina* or divine reading. *Lectio divina* is prayer over the Scriptures.

The first element of this type of prayer is reading *(lectio):* you take a short passage from the Bible, preferably a Gospel passage and read it carefully, perhaps three or more times. Let it really soak-in.

The second element is meditation *(meditatio).* By using your imagination enter into the Biblical scene in order to "see" the setting, the people, and the unfolding action. It is through this meditation that you encounter the text and discover its meaning for your life.

The next element is prayer *(oratio)* or your personal response to the text: asking for graces, offering praise or thanksgiving, seeking healing or forgiveness. In this prayerful engagement with the text, you open yourself up to the possibility of contemplation.

Contemplation *(contemplatio)* is a gaze turned toward Christ and the things of God. By God's action of grace, you may be raised above meditation to a state of seeing or experiencing the text as mystery and reality. In contemplation, you come into an experiential contact with the One behind and beyond the text.

Further Reading and Additional Resources:

on the Catholic Faith:

The Navarre Bible volumes

The Spiritual Exercises of St. Ignatius transl. by Louis J. Puhl, S.J.

The Catechism of the Catholic Church, Second Edition

ccc.usccb.org/flipbooks/catechism/files/assets/basic-html/page-I.html

www.usccb.org/about/divine-worship/liturgical-calendar/upload/2020cal.pdf

usccb.org/bible (can be clicked on for "today's readings," as well as easily navigable for references herein)

on Vipassana Buddhism, Mindfulness Meditation, and the Noble Eightfold Path:

Mindfulness in Plain English by Bhante Gunaratana

The 4 Foundations of Mindfulness in Plain English by Bhante Gunaratana

8 Mindfulness Steps to Happiness: Walking the Buddha's Path by Bhante Gunaratana

Beyond Mindfulness in Plain English by Bhante Gunaratana

Daily Prayers

Morning Offering

(prayers of gratitude and openness)

i.e the prayer of Thomas Merton

My Lord God, I have no idea where I am going. I do not see the road ahead of me. I cannot know for certain where it will end, nor do I really know myself, and the fact that I think that I am following your will does not mean that I am actually doing so. But I believe that the desire to please you does in fact please you. And I hope that I have that desire in all that I am doing. I hope that I will never do anything apart from that desire. And I know that if I do this you will lead me by the right road, though I may know nothing about it. Therefore I will trust you always though I may seem to be lost and in the shadow of death. I will not fear, for you are ever with me, and you will never leave me to face my perils alone.

another prayer of Morning Offering:

O Jesus, through the Immaculate Heart of Mary, I offer you my prayers, works, joys, and sufferings of this day for all the intentions of your Sacred Heart. In union with the Holy Sacrifice of the Mass throughout the world for the salvation of souls, the reparation for sins, the reunion of all, and in particular for the intentions of the Holy Father this month.

Memorare

Remember,
O most gracious Virgin Mary,
that never was it known
that anyone
who fled to your protection,
implored your help, or
sought your intercession
was left unaided.
Inspired by this confidence,
I fly unto you,
O Virgin of Virgins, my mother.
To you I come,
before you I stand,
sinful and sorrowful.
O mother of the world incarnate,
despise not my petitions,
but in your mercy,
hear me and answer me.
Amen.

Nicene Creed

I believe in one God,
the Father almighty,
maker of heaven and earth,
of all things visible and invisible.
I believe in one Lord Jesus Christ,
the Only Begotten Son of God,
born of the Father before all ages.
God from God, Light from Light,
true God from true God,
begotten, not made, consubstantial with the Father,
through him all things were made.
For our men and for our salvation
he came down from heaven,
and by the Holy Spirit was incarnate of the Virgin Mary,
and became man.
For our sake he was crucified under Pontius Pilate,
he suffered death and was buried,
and rose again on the third day
in accordance with the Scriptures.
He ascended into heaven
and is seated at the right hand of the Father.
He will come again in glory
to judge the living and the dead
and his kingdom will have no end.
I believe in the Holy Spirit, the Lord, the giver of life,
who proceeds from the Father and the Son,
who with the Father and the Son is adored and glorified,
who has spoken through the prophets.

I believe in one, holy, catholic, and apostolic church.
I confess one Baptism for the forgiveness of sins --
and I look forward to the resurrection of the dead
and the life of the world to come.
Amen.

Our Father

Our Father, who art in heaven,
hallowed be thy name.
Thy kingdom come.
They will be done, on earth, as it is in heaven.
Give us this day our daily bread,
and forgive us our trespasses, as we forgive those who trespass against us,
and lead us not into temptation, but deliver us from evil.
Amen.

Hail Mary

Hail Mary, full of grace, the Lord is with thee.
Blessed art thou among women
and blessed is the fruit of thy womb, Jesus.
Holy Mary, Mother of God,
pray for us sinners, now, and at the hour of our death.
Amen.

Glory Be (Doxology)

Glory be to the Father,
and to the Son,
and to the Holy Spirit,
as it was in the beginning,
is now, and ever shall be
world without end. Amen.

Act of Contrition

Oh my God, I am sorry for my sins. In choosing to sin and failing to do good.
I firmly intend with the help of your son and the church, to make up for my
sins and to love as I should. Amen.

Blessings and Thanksgivings
before each meal

What Blessings do you use for each meal? Write them in here.

Evening Offering
(prayers of Thanksgiving and adoration)
What Evening Offerings befit you? Write them in here.

2020

Cycle B (96 Days)

ZEROTH WEEK

Define your "Lenten Mission"

What's the Objective? What's the point? What's the Goal? Why?
What are you going to do about it?

Research & Reflect on your Lenten Mission and Easter experience.

Develop a practice that works best for you to concentrate on the Purification of your mind, body, and heart, so as to invite God's Love and the fruits and graces of the Holy Spirit into your life.

Shrove Tuesday February 25th

Jas 4:1-10/Mk 9:30-37 (342)

Celebrate "Mardi Gras," "Carnival," "Pancake Tuesday," etc. with a King's Cake!

Indulge in wild times of over-the-top feasting (within a wholesome discipline, of course). Incorporate great music, costuming and masquerading, and (moderate) revelry.

Experience the effervescent joys of life in abundance, shared with community.

FIRST WEEK

Day 1

Ash Wednesday February 26th

Jl 2:12-18/2 Cor 5:20—6:2/Mt 6:1-6, 16-18 (219) Pss IV

Today marks the beginning of Lent!

Make this a Retreat day: take the day "off" if you can, or at least a half-day!

Attend Mass to receive the Ashes; you may choose to attend Daily Mass throughout Lent, in whichever capacity works well for your life and schedule.

Observe the Liturgy of the Hours, if possible:

Lauds (Morning Prayer)
Daytime Prayer (Terce/ mid-morning prayer); Sext (mid-day prayer); and Non (mid-afternoon prayer)
Vespers (Evening prayer)
Compline (Night prayer)

Read the Passion Narratives:

Matthew 26ff
Mark 14ff
Luke 22ff
John 11:45ff

Reflect, write, synthesize on what you have read and experienced today (as well as on Mardi Gras, comparative appreciation).

Concentrate on your objectives for this Lenten and Easter Season; align to the goals in mind and heart.

15 minutes of meditation

notes for February 26th, continued

Day 2

Thursday, February 27th

Dt 30:15-20/Lk 9:22-25 (220)

Contemplate The Genealogy of Jesus

15 minutes of meditation

List all your current relationships, by title not specific names
List all your past relationships, by title not specific names
List all your potential relationships, by title not specific names

Day 3

1st Friday of Lent February 28th

Is 58:1-9a/Mt 9:14-15 (221)

Daily Mass

15 minutes of meditation

1 hour writing (synthesis of learnings/ key insights)

Walk the Stations of the Cross at your local church; after, pray a rosary, and meditate on the perspective of Mary, as Mother, and that of Saint Joseph.

notes for February 28th, continued

notes for February 28th, continued

Day 4

Saturday, February 29th (Leap Day!)
Is 58:9b-14/Lk 5:27-32 (222)

Contemplate The Birth of Jesus

Practice quality time with children by employing the techniques of right thinking (intention), right action, right effort, and right mindfulness throughout every interaction.

Pay attention to the good things that are happening in your world, especially those you are directly experiencing. Share news of good observations, secular in nature, with others in an authentic and genuine way.

Stewardship-in-action! (give 2-4 hours of your time out-in-the-world-at-large) for other beings in your community, city, spheres of influence....

15 minutes of meditation

SECOND WEEK

Day 5

1st Sunday of Lent March 1st

Gn 2:7-9; 3:1-7/Rom 5:12-19 or 5:12, 17-19/Mt 4:1-11 (22) Pss I

Sunday Mass Celebration
Day of Rest and Fellowship
Nourishment: meals and relationships

15 minutes of meditation

Physical exercises: 50-minutes of fresh well-oxygenated air around trees, yoga, sit-ups, dancing, swimming laps, running, bicycling, walking, cardiovascular activity

Day 6

Monday, March 2nd

Lv 19:1-2, 11-18/Mt 25:31-46 (224)

Contemplate The Visit of the Magi

Practice quality time with elders by employing the techniques of right thinking (intention), right action, right effort, right mindfulness throughout every interaction.

Consider The Gifts of the Holy Spirit (7). The traditional list of these seven gifts is derived from Isaiah 11:1-3.

They are wisdom, understanding, knowledge, counsel, piety, fortitude, and awesome respect of the Lord.

How are they present throughout the lives of you and your loved ones?

Record and share these insights.

Consider The Fruits of the Holy Spirit (12).

The fruits are perfections that the Holy Spirit forms in us as the "first fruits of eternal glory."

The tradition of the Church lists twelve of them: charity, joy, peace, patience, kindness, goodness, generosity, gentleness, faithfulness, modesty, self-control, and chastity.

How are they present throughout the lives of you and your loved ones?

Record and share these insights.

Consider the 5 pillars of Islam and how these "pillars" share similarities with Catholicism.

15 minutes of meditation

Day 7

Tuesday, March 3rd

Is 55:10-11/Mt 6:7-15 (225)

contemplate The Flight to Egypt and The Massacre of the Infants

Practice dialogue with someone else. Practice deep listening and appreciative inquiry. Practice authentic learning from "opposing" points of view. After, upon reflection, synthesize how dialogue can bring you together by integrating both previously differing -and- complementary perspectives to enrich your whole life with God's Love.

15 minutes of meditation

Day 8

Wednesday, March 4th

Jon 3:1-10/Lk 11:29-32 (226)

Contemplate The Return from Egypt

Focus on being together (reuniting) with loved ones, connecting meaningfully, and participating in meaningful activities.

15 minutes of meditation

Day 9

Thursday, March 5th
Est C:12, 14-16, 23-25/Mt 7:7-12 (227)

Contemplate The Preaching of John the Baptist
and The Baptism of Jesus

Consider and learn about Jewish rites and customs and how these
lay the foundations for and share similarities with traditions and
observances of the Catholic Church. If possible, make plans with a
Jewish friend to graciously attend Seder (Passover dinner) this year.

15 minutes of meditation

Day 10

2nd Friday of Lent March 6th

Ez 18:21-28/Mt 5:20-26 (228)

Daily Mass

15 minutes of meditation

1 hour writing (synthesis of learnings/ key insights)

notes for March 6th, continued

notes for March 6th, continued

notes for March 6th, continued

Day 11

Saturday, March 7th

Dt 26:16-19/Mt 5:43-48 (229)

Contemplate The Temptation of Jesus

Trust-in-action! (give 2-4 hours of your time out-in-the-world-at-large) to build, maintain, encourage, teach, learn... how to trust with other beings in your community, city, spheres of influence...

15 minutes of meditation

THIRD WEEK

Day 12

2nd Sunday of Lent March 8th

Gn 12:1-4a/2 Tm 1:8b-10/Mt 17:1-9 (25) Pss II

Sunday Mass Celebration
Day of Rest and Fellowship
Nourishment: meals and relationships

15 minutes of meditation

Physical exercises: 50-minutes of fresh well-oxygenated air around trees, yoga, sit-ups, dancing, swimming laps, running, bicycling, walking, cardiovascular activity

Day 13

Monday, March 9th (Full Moon)

Dn 9:4b-10/Lk 6:36-38 (230)

Contemplate The Beginning of the Galilean Ministry and The Call of the First Disciple

Offer your prayers for those embarking on the call to Holy Orders (priesthood, other orders).

15 minutes of meditation

Day 14

Tuesday, March 10th

Is 1:10, 16-20/Mt 23:1-12 (231)

Contemplate Ministering to a Great Multitude
Offer your prayers for the Lay Faithful.

15 minutes of meditation

Wednesday, March 11th

Jer 18:18-20/Mt 20:17-28 (232)

Contemplate The Sermon on the Mount
Pray for our Holy Guardian Angels

15 minutes of meditation

Day 16

Thursday, March 12th

Jer 17:5-10/Lk 16:19-31 (233)

Contemplate The Beatitudes

Pray for the Communion of Saints.

Perhaps, study a specific subset of Saints. At this time in your life, with whom do you most resonate? Why?

15 minutes of meditation

Day 17

3rd Friday of Lent March 13th

Gn 37:3-4, 12-13a, 17b-28a/Mt 21:33-43, 45-46 (234)

Consider the alchemical process of turning our agony into celebration.

Daily Mass

15 minutes of meditation

1 hour writing (synthesis of learnings/ key insights)

notes for March 13th, continued

notes for March 13th, continued

Day 18

Saturday, March 14th

Mi 7:14-15, 18-20/Lk 15:1-3, 11-32 (235)

Contemplate The Similes of Salt and Light

Kindness-in-action! (Give 2-4 hours of your time out-in-the-world-at-large) to engender kindness with other beings in your community, city, spheres of influence...

15 minutes of meditation

FOURTH WEEK

Day 19

3rd Sunday of Lent March 15th

Ex 17:3-7/Rom 5:1-2, 5-8/Jn 4:5-42 or 4:5-15, 19b-26, 39a, 40-42 (28) Pss III

Sunday Mass Celebration
Day of Rest and Fellowship
Nourishment: meals and relationships

15 minutes of meditation

Physical exercises: 50-minutes of fresh well-oxygenated air around trees, yoga, sit-ups, dancing, swimming laps, running, bicycling, walking, cardiovascular activity

Day 20

Monday, March 16th
2 Kgs 5:1-15b/Lk 4:24-30 (237)

Contemplate Teaching about Law

Practice living according to The Noble Eightfold Path.
i.e. "The Right[eous] Path" (the Way, the Truth, and the Light)
and how the 3-parts of practicing Harmony in your own personal
life can bring about Peace through the higher art of God's Love.

Purify your thoughts = Right Thoughts, Right Intentions

Purify your speech by purifying your words and choice of language
= Right Truth (kind, truthful, beneficial)

Purify your actions to better align with your intentions = Right
Action

15 minutes of meditation

Day 21

Tuesday, March 17th (St. Patrick's Day)
Dn 3:25, 34-43/Mt 18:21-35 (238)

Contemplate Teaching about Anger

Practice mini-meditations throughout this day as a way of continuous recalibration, centering, and alignment. Set a chime on your watch on the 12th-minute of every hour to breathe. Inhale wholly to smell the spectrum; exhale completely.

15 minutes of meditation

Day 22

Wednesday, March 18th

Dt 4:1, 5-9/Mt 5:17-19 (239)

Contemplate Teaching about Adultery and Teaching about Divorce

"Love me for who I am; let me be loved as I am."

Journal for 8 minutes about what the most exemplary love looks like to you. Day 1 of 8

15 minutes of meditation

Day 23

Thursday, March 19th
(Solemnity, Feast Day of St. Joseph)

2 Sm 7:4-5a, 12-14a, 16/Rom 4:13, 16-18, 22/Mt 1:16, 18-21, 24a or Lk 2:41-51a (543) Pss Prop

Attend Daily Mass in honor of Saint Joseph; pray about Saint Joseph and his relationships and roles.

Journal for 8 minutes about what the most exemplary love looks like to you. Day 2 of 8

Contemplate Teaching about Oaths

15 minutes of meditation

Day 24

4th Friday of Lent March 20th
(the Vernal Equinox: 1st Day of Spring)
Hos 14:2-10/Mk 12:28-34 (241)

Consider the alchemical process of turning death into the renewal of life.

Daily Mass

15 minutes of meditation

1 hour writing (synthesis of learnings/ key insights)

notes for March 20th, continued

notes for March 20th, continued

Day 25

Saturday, March 21st

Hos 6:1-6/Lk 18:9-14 (242)

Contemplate Teaching about Retaliation

Faithfulness-and-Adoration-for-God-in-action! (Give 2-4 hours of your time out-in-the-world-at-large) to share your experience of deep faith and adoration with other beings in your community, city, spheres of influence....

15 minutes of meditation

FIFTH WEEK

Day 26

4th Sunday of Lent March 22nd

1 Sm 16:1b, 6-7, 10-13a/Eph 5:8-14/Jn 9:1-41 or 9:1, 6-9, 13-17, 34-38 (31) Pss IV

Sunday Mass Celebration
Day of Rest and Fellowship
Nourishment: meals and relationships

15 minutes of meditation

Physical exercises: 50-minutes of fresh well-oxygenated air around trees, yoga, sit-ups, dancing, swimming laps, running, bicycling, walking, cardiovascular activity

Monday, March 23rd
Is 65:17-21/Jn 4:43-54 (244)

Contemplate Love of Enemies
Practice Right Speech.
Ask yourself before speaking,

"Is it true? Is it correct? Is it uplifting? Is it kind? Is it beneficial? Is it timely? Is it welcome? Is it gentle? Is it moderate (useful, meaningful, harmonious)?"

Perhaps, speech is not what we have known it to be. Practice soft words, silence, and the tone throughout all your communications, when most appropriate. Practice mindfulness of Right Speech.

15 minutes of meditation

Day 28

Tuesday, March 24th (New Moon)
Ez 47:1-9, 12/Jn 5:1-16 (245)

Contemplate Teaching about Almsgiving
Practice the art of giving, tithing, and generosity with grace.

Journal for 8 minutes about what the most exemplary love looks like to you. Day 3 of 8

15 minutes of meditation

Wednesday, March 25th (Solemnity, the Annunciation)

Is 7:10-14; 8:10/Heb 10:4-10/Lk 1:26-38 (545) Pss Prop

Contemplate Teaching about Prayer

Focus on your carriage and posture throughout this day; i.e. the "lifting up of our hearts."

Journal for 8 minutes about what the most exemplary love looks like to you. Day 4 of 8

15 minutes of meditation

Day 30

Thursday, March 26th

Ex 32:7-14/Jn 5:31-47 (247)

Contemplate The Lord's Prayer

Practice loving-kindness, compassion, appreciative joy, and equanimity.

Begin the process of preparing your heart for forgiveness and reconciliation. Begin to list (mentally or explicitly) those things for which you wish to be forgiven. Note on your calendar when you can attend the Sacrament of Reconciliation this season.

Journal for 8 minutes about what the most exemplary love looks like to you. Day 5 of 8

15 minutes of meditation

Day 31

5th Friday of Lent March 27th

Wis 2:1a, 12-22/Jn 7:1-2, 10, 25-30 (248)

Consider the alchemical process of turning our sufferings into true and enduring joy.

Daily Mass

15 minutes of meditation

1 hour writing (synthesis of learnings/ key insights)

notes for March 27th, continued

notes for March 27th, continued

Day 32

Saturday, March 28th

Jer 11:18-20/Jn 7:40-53 (249)

Contemplate Teaching about Fasting

Willingness-for-God's-work-in-action! (Give 2-4 hours of your time out-in-the-world-at-large) to experience your willingness to do the work that God calls upon you to do by giving your talents for the betterment of other beings in your community, city, spheres of influence....

15 minutes of meditation

SIXTH WEEK

Day 33

5th Sunday of Lent March 29th

Ez 37:12-14/Rom 8:8-11/Jn 11:1-45 or 11:3-7, 17, 20-27, 33b-45 (34) Pss I

Sunday Mass Celebration
Day of Rest and Fellowship
Nourishment: meals and relationships

15 minutes of meditation

Physical exercises: 50-minutes of fresh well-oxygenated air around trees, yoga, sit-ups, dancing, swimming laps, running, bicycling, walking, cardiovascular activity

Day 34

Monday, March 30th

Dn 13:1-9, 15-17, 19-30, 33-62 or 13:41c-62/Jn 8:1-11 (251)

Contemplate Treasure in Heaven

Practice loving-kindness, compassion, appreciative joy, and equanimity throughout the day.

Continue the list you began in regards to those things for which you wish to be forgiven and bring to the priest. Continue to prepare your heart, wholly, for the Sacrament of Reconciliation.

Journal for 8 minutes about what the most exemplary love looks like to you. Day 6 of 8

15 minutes of meditation

Day 35

Tuesday, March 31st

Nm 21:4-9/Jn 8:21-30 (252)

Contemplate The Light of the Body

Practice loving-kindness, compassion, appreciative joy, and equanimity throughout the day.

Continue the list you began in regards to those things for which you wish to be forgiven and bring to the priest. Continue to prepare your heart, wholly, for the Sacrament of Reconciliation and the Salvation of sincere remorse (the balm of healing that accompanies the Freedom we receive through these sacred and blessed acts).

Journal for 8 minutes about what the most exemplary love looks like to you. Day 7 of 8

15 minutes of meditation

Day 36

Wednesday, April 1st (April Fools' Day)

Dn 3:14-20, 91-92, 95/Jn 8:31-42 (253)

Contemplate God and Money

Have fun!

Create and/or participate in wholesome opportunities for sincere laughter!

15 minutes of meditation

Day 37

Thursday, April 2nd

Gn 17:3-9/Jn 8:51-59 (254)

Contemplate Dependence on God

Meditation on the path to forgiveness (both received and given), Reconciliation, and Salvation. Practice perpetual forgiveness and mindfulness.

Develop some "Letting Go exercises" of your choosing; take notes of your evolving practice of "letting go" to allow space for God to bless us. For example, your practice may include playing your favorite music, instruments, singing, or dancing (rejoicing with the wavelengths that allow you to access greater joy). Do whatever allows you to let energy (of all kinds) flow more easily without worry, fear, anxiety, or doubt.

Reflect on how everything to-date ties into the Moral Teachings of Jesus particularly with emphasis on God's Love within our humanity.

Journal for 8 minutes about what the most exemplary love looks like to you. Day 8 of 8

15 minutes of meditation

Day 38

6th Friday of Lent April 3rd
Jer 20:10-13/Jn 10:31-42 (255)

Daily Mass

15 minutes of meditation

1 hour writing (synthesis of learnings/ key insights)

Walk the stations of the cross at your local church; pray a rosary after. Meditate on the shroud of Turin.

notes for April 3rd, continued

notes for April 3rd, continued

Day 39

Saturday, April 4th

Ez 37:21-28/Jn 11:45-56 (256)

Contemplate Judging Others

Offer your prayers for the life, story, soul, and lessons of The Good Thief.

15 minutes of meditation

SEVENTH WEEK

Day 40

Palm Sunday April 5th
(Passion Sunday; begins Holy Week)

Mt 21:1-11 (37)/Is 50:4-7/Phil 2:6-11/Mt 26:14—27:66 or 27:11-54 (38) Pss II

Sunday Mass Celebration
Day of Rest and Fellowship
Nourishment: meals and relationships

15 minutes of meditation

Physical exercises: 50-minutes of fresh well-oxygenated air around trees, yoga, sit-ups, dancing, swimming laps, running, bicycling, walking, cardiovascular activity

Day 41

Monday, April 6th

Is 42:1-7/Jn 12:1-11 (257)

Contemplate Pearls before Swine

15 minutes of meditation

Tuesday, April 7th (Full Moon)
Is 49:1-6/Jn 13:21-33, 36-38 (258)

Contemplate The Answer to Prayers

15 minutes of meditation

Day 43

Wednesday, April 8th
(The Buddha's Birthday; Passover begins)
Is 50:4-9a/Mt 26:14-25 (259)

Contemplate The Golden Rule and The Narrow Gate

15 minutes of meditation

Day 44

Holy Thursday April 9th

Chrism Mass: Is 61:1-3a, 6a, 8b-9/Rv 1:5-8/Lk 4:16-21 (260)

Evening Mass of the Lord's Supper: Ex 12:1-8, 11-14/1 Cor 11:23-26/Jn 13:1-15 (39)

Contemplate False Prophets
Contemplate The True Disciple and The Two Foundations

Ask questions. Especially those that seek to understand the pervasiveness of "suffering" throughout humanity. Uniquely revealing are those that begin with "why," in regards to the circumstances of these most holy events and stories.

For example, *"Why the time between Passover & Holy Thursday, and in what ways are they 'the same?'"*

15 minutes of meditation

Day 45

Good Friday April 10th

Is 52:13—53:12/Heb 4:14-16; 5:7-9/Jn 18:1—19:42 (40) Pss Prop

Retreat day: take the day "off" if you can.
Abstain from noise i.e. heavy motors, electronics.
Find a place of solitude, peace, and quiet; at minimum the hours between noon and 3 o'clock.
Observe the precepts of peace in your heart, mind, body.

Re-read the Passion Narratives:
Matthew 26ff, Mark 14ff, Luke 22ff, John 11:45ff

Matthew 27:57-61 When it was evening, there came a rich man from Arimathea named Joseph, who was himself a disciple of Jesus. He went to Pilate and asked for the body of Jesus; then Pilate ordered it to be handed over. Taking the body, Joseph wrapped it [in] clean linen and laid it in his new tomb that he had hewn in rock. Then he rolled a huge stone across the entrance to the tomb and departed. But Mary Magdalene and the other Mary remained sitting there, facing the tomb.

Mark 15:42-47 When it was already evening, since it was the day of preparation, the day before the sabbath, Joseph of Arimathea, a distinguished member of the council, who was himself awaiting the kingdom of God, came and courageously went to Pilate and asked for the body of Jesus. Pilate was amazed that he was already dead. He summoned the centurion and asked him if Jesus had already died. And when he learned of it from the centurion, he gave the body to Joseph. Having bought a linen cloth, he took him down, wrapped him in the linen cloth and laid him in a tomb that had been hewn out of the rock. Then he rolled a stone against the entrance to the tomb. Mary Magdalene and Mary the mother of Joses watched where he was laid.

Luke 23:50-56 Now there was a virtuous and righteous man named Joseph who, though he was a member of the council, had not consented to their plan of action. He came from the Jewish town of Arimathea and was awaiting the kingdom of God. He went to Pilate and asked for the body of Jesus. After he had taken the body down, he wrapped it in linen cloth and laid him in a rock-hewn tomb in which no one had yet been buried. It was the day of preparation, and the sabbath was about to begin. The women who had come from Galilee with him followed behind, and when they had seen the tomb and the way in which his body was laid in it, they returned and prepared spices and perfumed oils. Then they rested on the sabbath according to the commandment.

John 19:38-42 After this, Joseph of Arimathea secretly a disciple of Jesus for fear of the Jews, asked Pilate if he could remove the body of Jesus. And Pilate permitted it. So he came and took his body. Nicodemus, the one who had first come to him in the night, also came bringing a mixture of myrrh and aloes weighing about one hundred pounds. They took the body of Jesus and bound it with burial cloths along with the spices, according to Jewish custom. Now in the place where he had been crucified there was a garden, and in the garden a new tomb, in which no one had yet been buried. So they laid Jesus there because of the Jewish preparation day; for the tomb was close by.

Contemplate the agony of these final hours and the passions endured.

Contemplate the joy of giving up our own sufferings.

Optional: Listen to Andrew Lloyd Webber's Jesus Christ Superstar (but, of course, *all* of this curriculum is optional!)

Daily Mass

15 minutes of meditation

1 hour writing (synthesis of learnings/ key insights)

notes for April 10th, continued

notes for April 10th, continued

notes for April 10th, continued

notes for April 10th, continued

notes for April 10th, continued

Saturday, April 11th

Easter Vigil: Gn 1:1—2:2 or 1:1, 26-31a/Gn 22:1-18 or 22:1-2, 9a, 10-13, 15-18/ Ex 14:15—15:1/Is 54:5-14/Is 55:1-11/Bar 3:9-15, 32—4:4/Ez 36:16-17a, 18-28/ Rom 6:3-11/Mt 28:1-10 (41) Pss Prop

Contemplate The Cleansing of a Leper and The Healing of the Centurion's Servant

The concept of Resurrection suggests that there is no necessity for one's original body nor of our blood (per our earthly understanding of its uses). There is a "glorification" (thorough purification) of both body and blood. The Apostles (first Disciples) were given the body and blood of Christ at the Last Supper by Chirst himself before the day of his crucifixion. Although seemingly a symbolic offering, these actions presented greater spiritual significance and has become central to the celebration of Catholic Mass as the Eucharist -- meaning our most profound "Thanksgiving." How might all of this (in consideration of today's contemplations) be illuminating on various levels to you?

15 minutes of meditation

EIGHTH WEEK

Day 47

Easter Sunday April 12th
(1st Sunday of Easter)

Acts 10:34a, 37-43/Col 3:1-4 or 1 Cor 5:6b-8/Jn 20:1-9 (42) or Mt 28:1-10 (41) or, at an afternoon or evening Mass, Lk 24:13-35 (46) Pss Prop

The Octave of Easter
Sunday Mass Celebration
Day of Rest and Fellowship
Nourishment: meals and relationships

15 minutes of meditation

Physical exercises: 50-minutes of fresh well-oxygenated air around trees, yoga, sit-ups, dancing, swimming laps, running, bicycling, walking, cardiovascular activity

Today, I appreciate with gratitude:

_____

Day 48

Monday, April 13th

This week, read Revelation (as much aloud as you can), note (also, if you can) elements that might actually be calling upon our deepest wellsprings of God's Love and of being of One Body in this shared pursuit of Everlasting Life together with all beings.

15 minutes of meditation

Today, the focus of my journey is:

_____

Day 49

Tuesday, April 14th

Revelation

15 minutes of meditation

Today, I will let go and give over to the Holy Spirit, Saints, and Guardian Angels:

_____

Day 50

Wednesday, April 15th

Revelation

15 minutes of meditation

Today, the greatest Blessings present in my life are:

_____

Day 51

Thursday, April 16th (Passover ends)

Revelation

15 minutes of meditation

Today, I will let go and give over to Christ of the suffering of:

_____

Day 52

Friday, April 17th

Revelation

15 minutes of meditation

1 hour writing (synthesis of learnings/ key insights)

Today, I will acknowledge and give visible recognition of my love to:

_____

notes for April 17th, continued

notes for April 17th, continued

Day 53

Saturday, April 18th

Do (part 1 of 2) work in the garden, outside, in the yard, outside of the house and home, weather permitting.

15 minutes of meditation

Today, I will give my talents to:

_____

NINTH WEEK

Day 54

2nd Sunday of Easter April 19th

Acts 2:42-47/1 Pt 1:3-9/Jn 20:19-31 (43) Pss Prop

Sunday Mass Celebration
Day of Rest and Fellowship
Nourishment: meals and relationships

15 minutes of meditation

Physical exercises: 50-minutes of fresh well-oxygenated air around trees, yoga, sit-ups, dancing, swimming laps, running, bicycling, walking, cardiovascular activity

Today, I appreciate with gratitude:

_____

Day 55

Monday, April 20th

chapters 1-9 of The Acts of the Apostles

This week, read chapters 1-9 of The Acts of the Apostles, note (if you can) Latin phrases that most resonate with you in regards to God's Love within our humanity.

15 minutes of meditation

Today, I will concentrate the Blessings in my life on:

_____

Day 56

Tuesday, April 21st

Acts

15 minutes of meditation

Today, I will demonstrate my deepening faith by:

_____

Day 57

Wednesday, April 22nd

Acts

15 minutes of meditation

Today, I will express my love by :

_____

Day 58

Thursday, April 23rd

Acts

15 minutes of meditation

Today, I will cultivate peace by:

_____

Day 59

Friday, April 24th

Acts

15 minutes of meditation

1 hour writing (synthesis of learnings/ key insights)

Today, I acknowledge the difficulties and challenges facing:

_____

notes for April 24th, continued

notes for April 24th, continued

Day 60

Saturday, April 25th

Do (part 2 of 2) of work in the garden, outside, in the yard, outside of the house and home, weather permitting.

15 minutes of meditation

Today, I will strengthen my life by:

_____

TENTH WEEK

Day 61

3rd Sunday of Easter April 26th
Acts 2:14, 22-33/1 Pt 1:17-21/Lk 24:13-35 (46) Pss III

Sunday Mass Celebration
Day of Rest and Fellowship
Nourishment: meals and relationships

15 minutes of meditation

Physical exercises: 50-minutes of fresh well-oxygenated air around trees, yoga, sit-ups, dancing, swimming laps, running, bicycling, walking, cardiovascular activity

Today, I appreciate with gratitude:

_____

Day 62

Monday, April 27th

This week, read chapters 10-19 of The Acts of the Apostles, note (if you can) Latin phrases that most resonate with you in regards to God's Love within our humanity.

15 minutes of meditation

Today, I observed the beauty of:

_____

Day 63

Tuesday, April 28th

Acts

15 minutes of meditation

Today, I experienced a moment of Peace while:

_____

Day 64

Wednesday, April 29th

Acts

15 minutes of meditation

Today, I learned by the example of:

_____

Day 65

Thursday, April 30th

Acts

15 minutes of meditation

Today, I will create a better experience of life for:

_____

Day 66

Friday, May 1st

Acts

15 minutes of meditation

1 hour writing (synthesis of learnings/ key insights)

Today, I will let go of the difficulties and challenges of:

_____

notes for May 1st, continued

notes for May 1st, continued

Day 67

Saturday, May 2nd

Do [in-house] housework, spring-cleaning (dust, pollen, old food-stuffs, outdated paperwork; clothes), weather permitting.

15 minutes of meditation

Today, I am at peace with:

_____

ELEVENTH WEEK

Day 68

4th Sunday of Easter May 3rd
Acts 2:14a, 36-41/1 Pt 2:20b-25/Jn 10:1-10 (49) Pss IV

Sunday Mass Celebration
Day of Rest and Fellowship
Nourishment: meals and relationships

15 minutes of meditation

Physical exercises: 50-minutes of fresh well-oxygenated air around trees, yoga, sit-ups, dancing, swimming laps, running, bicycling, walking, cardiovascular activity

Today, I appreciate with gratitude:

_____

Day 69

Monday, May 4th

This week read chapters 20-29 of The Acts of the Apostles, note (if you can) Latin phrases that most resonate with you in regards to God's Love within our humanity.

15 minutes of meditation

Today, I will express my love and appreciation to:

_____

Day 70

Tuesday, May 5th

Acts

15 minutes of meditation

Today, I will cultivate peace in my heart by:

_____

Day 71

Wednesday, May 6th

Acts

15 minutes of meditation

Today, I will lead by example by:

_____

Day 72

Thursday, May 7th

Acts

15 minutes of meditation

Today, I will practice courage and fortitude by:

_____

Day 73

Friday, May 8th

Acts

15 minutes of meditation

1 hour writing (synthesis of learnings/ key insights)

Today, I will share my awe with:

_____

notes for May 8th, continued

notes for May 8th, continued

Day 74

Saturday, May 9th

Practice your Way of Peace for 2020, through intentional and right action within your community.

15 minutes of meditation

Today, I will acknowledge the good work of:

_____

TWELFTH WEEK

Day 75

5th Sunday of Easter May 10th

Acts 6:1-7/1 Pt 2:4-9/Jn 14:1-12 (52) Pss I

Sunday Mass Celebration
Day of Rest and Fellowship
Nourishment: meals and relationships

15 minutes of meditation

Physical exercises: 50-minutes of fresh well-oxygenated air around trees, yoga, sit-ups, dancing, swimming laps, running, bicycling, walking, cardiovascular activity

Today, I appreciate with gratitude:

_____

Day 76

Monday, May 11th

15 minutes of meditation

Today, I appreciate with gratitude:

_____

Day 77

Tuesday, May 12th

15 minutes of meditation

Today, I appreciate with gratitude:

_____

Day 78

Wednesday, May 13th

15 minutes of meditation

Today, I appreciate with gratitude:

Day 79

Thursday, May 14th

15 minutes of meditation

Today, I appreciate with gratitude:

_____

Day 80

Friday, May 15th

15 minutes of meditation

1 hour writing (synthesis of learnings/ key insights)

Today, I appreciate with gratitude:

_____

notes for May 15th, continued

notes for May 15th, continued

Day 81

Saturday, May 16th

Practice your Way of Peace for 2020, through intentional and right action within your community.

15 minutes of meditation

Today, I appreciate with gratitude:

_____

THIRTEENTH WEEK

Day 82

6th Sunday of Easter May 17th

Acts 8:5-8, 14-17/1 Pt 3:15-18/Jn 14:15-21 (55) Pss II

Sunday Mass Celebration
Day of Rest and Fellowship
Nourishment: meals and relationships

15 minutes of meditation

Physical exercises: 50-minutes of fresh well-oxygenated air around trees, yoga, sit-ups, dancing, swimming laps, running, bicycling, walking, cardiovascular activity

Today, I appreciate with gratitude:

_____

Monday, May 18th

15 minutes of meditation

Today, I appreciate with gratitude:

_____

Day 84

Tuesday, May 19th

15 minutes of meditation

Today, I appreciate with gratitude:

_____

Day 85

Wednesday, May 20th

15 minutes of meditation

Today, I appreciate with gratitude:

_____

Day 86

The Ascension: Thursday May 21st

Acts 18:1-8/Jn 16:16-20 (294)

Attend Daily Mass.

15 minutes of meditation

Today, I appreciate with gratitude:

_____

Day 87

Friday, May 22nd

15 minutes of meditation

1 hour writing (synthesis of learnings/ key insights)

Today, I appreciate with gratitude:

_____

notes for May 22nd, continued

notes for May 22nd, continued

Day 88

Saturday, May 23rd

Practice your Way of Peace for 2020, through intentional and right action within your community.

15 minutes of meditation

Today, I appreciate with gratitude:

_____

FOURTEENTH WEEK

Day 89

7th Sunday of Easter May 24th
(The Ascension)
Acts 1:1-11/Eph 1:17-23/Mt 28:16-20 (58) Pss Prop

Sunday Mass Celebration
Day of Rest and Fellowship
Nourishment: meals and relationships

15 minutes of meditation

Physical exercises: 50-minutes of fresh well-oxygenated air around trees, yoga, sit-ups, dancing, swimming laps, running, bicycling, walking, cardiovascular activity

Today, I appreciate with gratitude:

_____

Day 90

Monday, May 25th

15 minutes of meditation

Today, I appreciate with gratitude:

_____

Day 91

Tuesday, May 26th

15 minutes of meditation

Today, I appreciate with gratitude:

_____

Day 92

Wednesday, May 27th

15 minutes of meditation

Today, I appreciate with gratitude:

_____

Day 93

Thursday, May 28th

15 minutes of meditation

Today, I appreciate with gratitude:

_____

Day 94

Friday, May 29th

15 minutes of meditation

1 hour writing (synthesis of learnings/ key insights)

Today, I appreciate with gratitude:

_____

notes for May 29th, continued

notes for May 29th, continued

Day 95

Saturday, May 30th

Practice your Way of Peace for 2020, through intentional and right action within your community.

15 minutes of meditation

Today, I appreciate with gratitude: _

_____

FIFTEENTH WEEK

Day 96

Pentecost Sunday (Whit Sunday) May 31st

Vigil: Gn 11:1-9 or Ex 19:3-8a, 16-20b or Ez 37:1-14 or Jl 3:1-5/ Rom 8:22-27/Jn 7:37-39 (62) or, for the Extended Vigil: Gn 11:1-9/Ex 19:3-8a, 16-20b/Ez 37:1-14/Jl 3:1-5/Rom 8:22-27/ Jn 7:37-39 (Lectionary for Mass Supplement, 62) Day: Acts 2:1-11/1 Cor 12:3b-7, 12-13/Jn 20:19-23 (63) Pss Prop

Sunday Mass Celebration!
Day of Rest and Fellowship
Nourishment: meals and relationships

15 minutes of meditation

Physical exercises: 50-minutes of fresh well-oxygenated air around trees, yoga, sit-ups, dancing, swimming laps, running, bicycling, walking, cardiovascular activity

Today, I appreciate with gratitude:

_____

END NOTES
PREVIOUS CONTEMPLATIONS to inspire and motivate for the LENTEN SEASON

FIRST WEEK (contemplations)

Cycle 1

"in fulfillment of the Scriptures."

Blessed are the _____.

Letting our Light shine before others which glorifies our heavenly Father. Matthew 5:14

Understand our Light. What gives us Light? Matthew 5:24

Reconcile with my "brother" and then give gifts.

How do we reconcile? What are the ways of true reconciliation when such vastly different ways of navigating life are present in the relationship?

Settle with your opponent; the gospel of Matthew claims - Again, how are we to actually go about doing this; especially when we are / feel "limited" in resources?

What does it mean to be "poor in spirit?" Should not we be rich in spirit? (Matthew 5:3)

This lesson on "oaths" fascinates me in that it shows how much may change everyday from our expectations and with "God's plan" -- I shouldn't promise to do anything (with anybody) "tomor-

row." Perhaps there are light commitments that can be made for work or for love, but mostly they are hollows -- this has "deep potential."

"Give to one who asks of you, and do not turn your back on one who wants to borrow." Matthew 5:42

"Love your enemies, and pray for those who persecute you." Matthew 5:44

"For where your treasure is, there also may your heart be." Matthew 6:21

"Can any of your worrying add a single moment to your life-span" ... O, you of little faith?" Matthew 6:27, 6:30

... "your heavenly Father knows that you need them all" Matthew 6:32

"Do not worry about tomorrow; tomorrow will take care of itself." Matthew 6:34

"and the measure by which you measure will be measured out to you." Matthew 7:2 ½

"know how to give good gifts to your children." Matthew 7:11 ½

"This is the law and the prophets" (The Golden Rule) Matthew 7:12 ½

The Narrow Gate Matthew 7:13

the types of foundations we build for

our houses - rains fell... and flood...

Why not build for flexibility or rain & flooding and the elements of God's creation.

The Moral Teachings of Jesus are such that -

Well, so far they seem metaphorical. They leave room for interpretation and a variety of applications. I have been entertaining more questions than answers and also I question the authorship and accuracy of Jesus' teachings. The authors of the gospels are good writers, but I suppose they are also not telling every story of Jesus' life.

For example, Jesus lived in Egypt, until after the death of Herod; what about this story?

Was this "Herod the Great?" Surely not because he died in 4 BC It must've been the 2nd Herod; "Herod Archelaus" -- and yes "indeed" upon further digging into studies; it is - and he died in 18 AD. So that means that Jesus spent his "formative" years in Egypt (NOT in Israel, Bethlehem, Nazareth, Galilee) as I have up-to-this-time imagined. What are the implications of all this missing-story? What context are we missing? What insights, relationships, learnings about the life of Jesus?

He didn't "go back home" to Joseph's workshop as a carpenter after he was born; but to Egypt. Why did Egypt provide protection from the jealousies of King Herod? That's a long way to travel "by foot;" maybe they went by sea; -- they could've likely traveled by caravan. They didn't return to Nazareth ("home") until Jesus was "a man" of 14 or so -- (no longer a boy) -- so this is all fascinating to me -- although it doesn't tell me much, at least not yet, about the Moral Teachings; nor God's love. This missing history/ chronology also seems important -- I see Matthew 2:22

about Herod, Archelaus, Galilee, Nazareth...

And then, what's this about "Jerusalem" -- and all.

All this context interests me! and I understand the curiosity propelling "Biblical studies" -- it's fascinating to piece through What was happening, and to consider Jesus growing up, maturing, and becoming a man during this time. This is during a time of Roman high days; after Caesar during the Great stretches. Why don't we study these periods together? They are separated in our history lessons except some cursory mention to the Tigris & Euphrates or to the Mediterranean Sea. But here, the importance of dynamics between Egypt, Italy (Rome), and the Middle East are crucial; it is the crux (pardon the pun) of much of our civilization; all of Christianity. And, if "love" is at the root of it, then Why have we undergone so many wars?

The primary moral teachings here are (I feel) must be embedded in CONTEXT. >>

I'm craving to learn more about the context, which was probably quite obvious to the authors' of the gospels and their audiences. The context was a "known" and assumed condition of the stories to them; fortunately we have some clues -- and it's well, "preserved" and relatively "recent history;" So, Jesus did all his work in 18 years or so. We can call it 20 years, but that's not as likely as 15. Another question is "how old was he when he gathered his first disciples and led the Sermon on the Mount?" My guess is 18/19. Meaning, he had about 15 years of teaching, Miracle Working, articulation, and the like.

The "Our Father" (The Lord's Prayer) is given to us within this first section. That's actually pretty incredible. Also we are taught to trust in God to provide for us. Therefore I wonder, "what are our prayers to consist of, then?" Forgiveness & Thanksgiving; -- why ask for our "daily bread" when we are told that the Lord already knows we need it??

There are often some mixed messages, and I don't understand them.

And, is Jesus only for "man" kind or is he also for women?

The presence of Mary of Magdalene suggests

... what?

I'm curious. And to me, that is enough at this first week of reflections on his Moral teachings, as I am thrilled by my "curiosities." Thank you, God. I look forward to enlightenment on these points.

FIRST WEEK (contemplations)

Cycle 2

"Peace be with you; [and] he showed them his hands and his side... 'Peace be with you.'... and when he said this, and he breathed on them and said 'Receive the holy Spirit. Whose sins you forgive are forgiven, and whose sins you retain are retained... 'Peace be with you'..."

Three times he said it; twice, he repeated it. -- John 20:19

What's also interesting to me is the use of myrrh TWICE during the Passion Narratives - the first time being in the cup (as a narcotic to relieve his pain) on the way to the cross - which he refused - the second time being when his body was brought down from the cross (because of Passover) by Joseph of Arimathea and prepared for burial "according to the Jewish burial custom" - Myrrh was prepared with aloes and other spices and burial clothes for him to be placed in a tomb in a garden. This interests me because we know that one of the nativity gifts he receives is myrrh -- (gold and frankincense) -- and it was likely not cheap and it was likely not an ever-present fixture, so I wonder if it was the very same as the gift he received from the magi.

Nicodemus and Joseph of Arimethea... these are characters of whom I am most curious.

"you will know the truth, and the truth will set you free" John 8:31

"I am the light of the word. Whoever follows me will not walk in darkness, but will have the light of life." John 8:12

Purification -- ointment >>

the washing of the feet,.. then the burial... there is this underlying theme of purification -- how does this tie in with Jewish custom?

And then "the New Commandment of John 13:31 --

"'love one another. As I have loved you, so you also should love one another."

So the question is (which is particularly relevant on the day I write this "Valentine's Day") What IS Love? How do we know love? What is pure love? What is true love? What is this love that Jesus (by his Father) alludes to. Do we know it? perhaps through him and his life's work... from all the previous chapters and verses of the gospels.?

Jesus knows this love because it comes from his Father. So, he was blessed among men. I don't think it's a stretch to claim that most men do not know a "healthy" love from their fathers - they are among the fortunate if they do. And many men may not even know the love from their mothers - a pure love without guilt or blame and hard pressings. So, PERHAPS, first we (if applicable) must strive to love our children - for it is by loving our children that they come to know 'love.' and that love is what they take out into their worlds. What does this expression look like, especially considering life's dynamic challenges.

Beyond the context of fatherhood or motherhood, one can (and must) reapply this concept elsewhere and everywhere - to a garden, to home, to work, to the things we've been given to steward, to the relationships we have been blessed with, to the trees and species that surround us - our owl friends, our spider friends, our bee friends...

In a way, we must become that source of love for others. Jesus asked us to be like him. Right? He didn't say - don't do as I've done or taught. He said (I think) look upon me - my words are the Father's words - be like me. Be like the Father! So, it's not "hubris" (or is it?) then to say, "hey, okay, I'll strive to do so as God does." "I'll try to understand the will of God, and do God's will." "Hey! I can love as God loves - I'll strive for that!" Of course, it is so difficult. I think "I hunger. My back hurts. My heart hurts. My feelings feel hurt. I am stressed. I am thirsty. I must file my taxes. I must save for retirement. I need to give good gifts that cost a lot. I want to go out and have fun. I want great transportation. I want to nourish my own home. I want to nourish my relationships - love, confidante, & best friends... etc., etc., etc." We have all these and so many more distractions. - Why then is God not distracted? Why is God not distracted from giving us an abundance of Love?!

We can learn to accept those Blessings (love) that we are given (graciously), and not judge or condemn because it isn't enough or we don't yet see how it is 'right.' Also, wherever we find ourselves judging that it isn't "enough" or how we'd 'prefer' it - then mark it mindfully, this could be a grand opportunity to better ourselves. If we are so wise to see our own faults, then that is also a gift! - we desire action, as a result of desiring to better ourselves, by recognizing and acknowledging our shortcomings, our weaknesses, our opportunities for growth & maturity. Action over thought. Action over words. Actions through forgiveness. In good moments, I see this. I saw this when I had to pause in life because I was humbled by the very real fundamental challenges present in my life - I didn't want them to 'interfere' with my thoughts - but, they were there, I couldn't ignore the hunger in my heart and body, I had to "let go" and "let flow" and then I learned, because I did, and I saw something. In all our most fundamental and simplest challenges there is learning - and it is there & then, when we paused and bowed to it, that

I saw something, also, But as soon as I flipped the page I forgot, but as soon as I admitted that I forgot I remembered! And this is what I thought, although the elocution will likely be imperfect. "If we all tried to do as Jesus did - wouldn't we be walking around eating fish, sitting on mountains, teaching, talking in parables, drinking wine..." or what??

And if so how would our economies function?

How would "anything ever get done'?"

ETC.

(Well, then I was washing my hands and I had this further thought)

We are all given slightly unique circumstances of birth: our homes, our families, our schools, our experiences, our bioregions, our cultures (our diets)... are therefore all slightly, at least, unique across the globe - quite unique. So if each & every person did exactly what Jesus DID within their unique circumstances - well, that WOULD actually be radical!

What might that look like?

Well, I would gather around friends very often. I would bless every meal - the grains, the meat, and the drinks within our cups - at every point of "nourishment" I'd recognize that that abundance came from the Earth, from God -- and then I would cling to nothing tangible -

I'd have one really nice tunic (John 19:23)

but for me in my unique circumstances what would that be-?

And one pair of sandals - eh?

but sandals that can walk on for hundreds of miles and climb mountains with and carry crosses with - and in Atlanta - What would those be for me -

And when I travel to the Pacific Northwest or London or France or New Zealand - what would those be for me? And when I work wherever else I've been blessed to work - what would those be for me?

And there were other things he carried,

he wore -

but they were few and numerable - and I could find a list of them in the gospels - and I could adapt them to my own unique circumstances - and then I could be like Jesus. - and I am a woman, and that's okay because... well, who were the first witnesses of his Resurrection - women were present throughout the gospels, in subtle ways, but very much present. So, that's also a unique circumstance - I wish I knew what the other elements of the stories were that were not recorded, or are not currently visible to me.

Even if we ALL were to strive to do exactly as Jesus would do (given our unique circumstances) we would still have a rich fabric/ tapestry of life, relationships - ...

The key here (perhaps) is to accept our uniqueness, to accept that our relationships differ, our experiences differ, our number of siblings differ, the money we were given (or not given) to become 'adults' differs - and we are not to judge that harshly - we are to embrace it and forgive the "trespassing." Everyone of us is along this Journey, once born into this one shared Life.

So, now I wonder - "what did Jesus DO?"

And for that, to discover, despite our limitations, we each have resources --

We have our own internal wisdom! >> My own heart. To love myself! To love myself first. To speak as if my word is Truth. To live as if my life is Light. To act as a daughter of God. Wow! How profound! How life-changing -- to embrace and have that level and depth of confidence -- that is something!

And I'd likely speak less and listen even more.

And I'd only DO when I was sure that I was DOing in accord.

FIRST WEEK (contemplations)
Cycle 3

The 40 days and 40 nights were immediately after John the Baptist had baptized Jesus to "fulfill all righteousness" - and the Spirit of God descended like a dove - and a voice from the heavens said, "This is my beloved Son, with whom I am well pleased." and that is when Jesus "was led by the Spirit into the desert to be tempted by the devil" - ! Righteousness is "moral conduct in conformity with God's will. The question is: what is God's will? And what are other questions that I've deeply or thoroughly had this past year - for which I have looked forward to this time of disciplined reflection? Here are some quotes from the hour of readings today that reach me in some way: "One does not live by bread alone, but by every word that comes forth from the mouth of God." "The people who sit in darkness have seen a great light, on those dwelling in a land overshadowed by death, light has arisen." "You are the light of the world. A city sitting on a mountain cannot be hidden Nor should one light a lamp and then put it under a bushel basket; it is set on a lampstand, where it gives light to all in the house. Just so, your light must shine before others, that they may see your good deeds and glorify your heavenly Father." - "leave your gift there at the altar, go first and be reconciled... and then come and offer your gift. Settle with your opponent quickly..." Teaching about oaths, Love of Enemies, Teaching about Almsgiving, Teaching about Prayer, Teaching about Fasting, Treasure in Heaven ! - What about the "Treasure in Heaven" (Matthew 6:19) teaching speaks to me so thoroughly? It hits upon a chord - something striking. What? Perhaps - to understand what these "treasures in heaven " are. What "treasures" can neither moth nor decay destroy? They are amazing and marvelous treasures, surely - and they are beyond the physical bounds of humanity and the world of earth as we know it. And... Q! Who is Q. ha. ha. ha. YAY! Ian Fleming took inspiration from the Bible, as did J.K. Rowling for Harry Potter ("unquenchable fire") Matthew 3:!2, and

Shakespeare.

Now, it is our moment.

Matthew 12:42 > and they shared among them the best of each one according to their own gifts and talents... And it shall be said, "because they came from the ends of the earth to hear the wisdom of Solomon, here, where they were. Oh little, little, sweet little children - all mature now - having become more graceful with time, yet still a child in the heart of God; a youthful child in so many ways, such a dear soul; a spirit of a holy wisdom. Now, matured into a true exemplar with God's Grace, - called upon to be a leader, a pillar of the community from each city set within the forest of the foothills of such great mountains."

These are such difficult, confusing, and mangled times. People are depressed, confused, bewildered, unhealthy - they make poor decisions, impoverished decision; their choices snowball into dire situations. They become saddled with the exponential growth of their sins - and they turn to drugs (prescription or other) or further wrongdoing. I fail and fall too; I'm not exempt. Vice has become normalized and accepted. Food & drink are contaminated, sold "fairly," and consumed widely - it leads to further suffering: cancers and painful death. Life has become a tangled mess of suffering - the path of God, the ways of God are hidden; even from well-intentioned souls. Dear Lord God, I pray for compassion (and self-love, kindness, and grace - the courage to shine my Light. The courage to to be a Light. And the wisdom to let God Guide me along his path & the Blessed way. A Refreshing History is in the midst of being written - not a History of who presided, who reigned - the Kings of England, the Popes of the Catholic Church, the battles fought. There is something else to be studied, to be learned, to be "storied," - something more important than "politics" or "government" - "For the kingdom of heaven is at hand!" Matthew 3:2 and then again and again. How are we each a part of the compre-

hensive story?

Instead of "memorizing politics and ancient histories" - what else is there to learn, to memorize? the ways and will of God! to understand how to BE more kind, more compassionate, more open, a stronger light, an instrument of Peace, worthy of God's Blessings. There is so much more to Life than studying the lineages and intermarriages of "royalty" of the monarchs of our ancestral lands. Those were flawed times with limited vision, as are all times. And yet, we are here now - what benefit can they grant us? What wisdom will they bestow us. What is the importance of knowing that James II (Roman Catholic preceding William of Orange) dropped the "Great Seal" in the Thames and fled for the protection of France? ... I have questions, but I can't even begin to formulate them all. Very little of this life even makes sense enough to me anymore to know where to begin. So maybe I should begin with God, the Holy Spirit, with trust in the Lord. Traffic doesn't make sense. Anger doesn't make sense. Buying things just to fill a void (huh.) doesn't make sense. There are voids everywhere. Perhaps even, purposefully, by God - the Tao - an empty vessel. But these 40 days and 40 nights are to take us to the brink of temptation so that we can feel the raw presence of the Holy Spirit. What good is my Lenten Mission? What am I even really doing? I'm not "giving up anything" - or maybe I am. I'm giving up my time - so that I can be in the presence of the "Word of God." But, it's a lot of work and a lot of time and also I feel confused, but less confused because I'm gaining in wisdom, in hope, in [good] words (I hope). My thoughts are becoming purified and clarified (I hope), but my body - What about my body? Except to say... my mind is my body; and my treasures shall be in Heaven. I suppose.

Disciples were needed because there was so much work to be done - and that at a time when the population of the earth was _____. (?) Populations... #s, politics, governance... what's it all saying? what's the teaching? what are "we" trying to learn by "studying scripture?" If these are all "teachings" and Jesus was called "Teacher," then what? for why? for what? He's not teaching them "history" per se. He's teaching them Wisdom - and wisdom is the conduct through which happiness and JOY come to life. Dreams are acknowledged and respected. They play a significant role. And yet "history" is alluded to - in order to build "credence." Or do I mean "authority" or like, justification or something to that effect. It's almost as if to say, sure - we have this "Old Testament" which is revered, and all these old kings and lineages and kingdoms and all, but here's what we do now about it all - "Do to others whatever you would have them do to you." The Golden Rule Matthew 7:12, and therein lies the precept of compassion - why? Why does this RULE take precedence over all others - why more important than anything else? Why? Perhaps because everything is connected; for every action there is an equal and opposite reaction" - perhaps because there is (are) a hidden force(s) determining how much happiness can be a part of our lives - like as in, casting our bread to the sea; and giving your light... Peace and Joy are Jesus' way; not battles and war - only through allegory are they brought in, only to relate - Are there any devout spiritual leaders of political boundaries? It's all FASCINATING. and I don't know much of anything. I'm just writing because that's what I'm "called upon" to do. Everything else is really quite beyond me, and I don't make sense of it, ... And I just REALLY feel the need to perpetually slow down, and breathe, and soak up my dreams, and reside in the breath of God and to learn from every moment of action and interaction; and just HOPE that I'm living an exemplary Life. Dear Lord God, I adore you. What am I questing to discover?

What did Jesus DO?

Teaching, healing, story-telling; these are things he did.

How did he exemplify living a good life?

"making a living?"

What about the economy? winemakers, growers of food, builders, carpenters, fishermen, glass makers; - how can 'these' people earn a living -AND- follow the Guidance of Jesus Christ?

Maybe; just perhaps, people choose professions that disallow them to integrate into the fabric of Christ's teachings. On Dear Lord God, tell me more! I am Yours. Why do people (I) sin? Why do people (I) make poor decisions? Why do people (I) complicate our lives and do harm? Why?! What are the underlying reasons why?!!? I.e. how did Jesus live for 30-something years! And not "earn-a-living?"

SECOND WEEK
(contemplations)
Cycle 1

The Mission of the Twelve

"you will be given at that moment what you are to say"

..."it is lawful to do good on the Sabbath"

"For from the fullness of the heart the mouth speaks.

A good person brings forth good out of a store of goodness,..."

The Purpose of the Parables

... understand with your heart

"twelve wicker baskets full"

"Take courage, it is I,"...

... "the things that come out from the mouth, come from the heart;"...

"gave thanks, broke the loaves, and gave them to the

disciples, who in turn gave them to the crowds."..

"will repay everyone according to his conduct."

"Rise, and do not be afraid."

The Parable of the Lost Sheep

Blessing of the Children

"send out angels with a trumpet blast, and they will

gather his elect from the four winds, from one end

of heaven to the other."

"but the wise brought flasks of oil for their lamps"

"Since you were faithful in small matters, I will

give you great responsibilities"

"whatever you did for one of these least brothers of mine,

you did for me."

"An alabaster jar of costly perfumed oil,..."

The Lord's Supper

... took bread, said the blessing, broke it, and gave it..."

"after singing a hymn..."

"The spirit is willing, but the flesh is weak."

"Put your sword back into its sheath, for all who take the sword will perish by the sword."

"For he knew that it was out of envy that they handed him over."

"Most blessed are you among women, and blessed is the fruit of your womb."

"And Mary kept all those things, reflecting on them in her heart."

"the boy Jesus"

"After three days they found him in the temple - sitting in the midst of the teachers, listening to them, and asking them questions,..."

"... his mother kept all these things in

her heart."

"when Jesus began his ministry he was about thirty years of age."

"one does not live by bread alone."

" 'He will command his angels concerning you, to guard you' and, with their hands they will support you, lest you dash your foot against a stone."

Love of enemies

"tunic"

"Do to others as you would have them do to you."

"But rather, love your enemies and do good to them,

And lend expecting nothing back; then your

reward will be"...

Judging Others

"For the measure by which you measure will in return be measured out to you."

"A good person out of the store of goodness in his heart produces good,..."

"who comes to me, listens to my words, and acts on them."

"Your faith has saved you; go in peace."

The Parable of the Lamp

"For there is nothing hidden that will not

become visible, and nothing secret that will not

be known and come to light. Take care then,

how you hear."

"So they set sail,"...

The Mission of the Twelve

"Take nothing for the journey, neither walking stick,

nor sack, nor food, nor money, and let no one take a

second tunic; Whatever house you enter, stay there and

leave from there."

The Transfiguration of Jesus

The Mission of the Seventy-two

Into whatever house you enter, first say,

"Peace to this household.' If a peaceful person lives here, your peace will rest on him; but if not it will return to you"

The Greatest Commandment

... "You shall love the Lord, your God, with all your heart, with all your being, with all your strength, and with all your mind, and your neighbor as yourself"...

... do this and you will live."

What is on my mind and in my heart during this Mission of this Lenten Season is >>>

love of my sister and brothers

forgiveness of my brothers and sisters, of all fellow passengers in this lifetime.

trusting in the Lord, my God, --

{write out a personal story, anecdote calling to mind how these Moral Teachings might become practical and applicable to our daily lives and [nourishing of healthy] relationships; state the story using facts and then write how that brought up certain emotions for you, then write compassionately from the other person's perspective. State the challenges. Explore the past and future expectations to show how that affects current dynamics. Explore how "love" (i.e. mercy, forgiveness, non-judgment can play a part in the healing? What other relationship-challenges do you face? In the past? In the present? What happened that makes that "love" difficult? How does it differ from "easy" love? What's entangled in it? What can you do differently, in each moment, to help shift that dynamic towards "heaven on earth?" What attributes does this person have that contribute to your life being better, more interesting, enriched, even if you dislike much about that person. What do you admire about this person whom you are challenged by? Their strengths of character, talents, gifts? How can you bring about peace when you are feeling most angered? What assumptions are working under the surface in your mind and heart? What are you clinging to that disallows reconciliation/ whole forgiveness to occur? What good can you do? What can you entrust to the Lord, God, after you've done your good work? In what ways have you been transformed by God's love, mercy, forgiveness of others towards you! when you have said or done wrong (and thus grown in love, maturity, and now wisdom)? What does it mean for

you to love and to be loved? How are those different with different people? How does love enrich your life? }

SECOND WEEK (contemplations)
Cycle 2

"You are the light of the world. A city set on a mountain cannot be hidden. Nor do they light a lamp and then put it under a bushel basket; it is set on a lampstand where it gives light to all the house. Just so, your light must shine before others, that they may see your good deeds and glorify your heavenly Father." Matthew 5:13-16

What is each, our, Light?

How do I replenish it? What is the fuel (like the beeswax)? What steadies the flame (like the wick)? A lamp that is lit needs good air-flow, but in too much wind it flickers and fusses and the light becomes difficult to be steadfast by -, So, too, must our lights be.

What has interested me since the 1st Friday of this Lenten season - are the years between Jesus' nativity in Bethlehem and his 'life work' in Nazareth, Galilee. Between that time, according to Matthew he was in Egypt - and I have heard near Cairo. And according to Luke, they returned once a year to Jerusalem for Jewish cultural traditions of Passover. Fascinating! ...

One of his teachings states clearly:

"know how to give good gifts to your children, how much more will your heavenly Father give good things to those who ask him." Matthew 7:11

Well, on that same way of thought I've found that the father's role in the family is a "moral learning" - the father's role being to give good gifts to his children and the way to do that, to be able to do that is to be present for them and in their lives; to watch them and appreciate their natural inclinations and talents - to witness their joys and what makes their hearts sing - as well as what can help that unique child grow - fostering their nourishment. It seems like the role of the father is to give good gifts to his children - and in so doing, he fashions the health of the family - for surely a good thoughtful father will make a fine husband - for also what better gift to give children than to live by example - and to exemplify that of being a good man to his woman. What is this example then? What do these actions look like? Well, to my understanding, they look a lot like the Moral Teachings of Jesus - how does one treat their fellow brothers and sisters, how does one participate in humankind? How does one help give confidence to others to bring forth each, their, own light?

Cleanliness! Washing of the Feet!!! It seems like "cleanliness" is a moral teaching in itself - just as too is that what we eat and drink! We see this in several circumstances - anointing and washing and good smells. And this is a topic of the Moral Teachings that I would like to learn more about with real context.

Giving without counting the cost.

But, what is said about giving of our time to help solve problems with others so that (a) they may learn from our light & talents, gifts, skills, experience and (b) that we may offer something to subdue the frustration of others which leads towards anger?

And then, when do we stop giving to others?

"Do to others whatever you would have them do to you." Matthew 7:12

In this way we are urged in one sentence to follow the law and the prophets: the wisdom and compassion. For, I believe, as I've explored previously, that we may all be "one body." (Catholic => Universal) - "whatsoever you do to the least of our brethren, that you do unto me" - in a way - it's like Systems Thinking. And the "Web of Life" - that we are actually One Body. That there

are these truths - mostly which he spoke in Parable - about who we are as one Super Organism. The earth, all its (her) inhabitants! Which is why it becomes even more important to care for that which is sick or ill or in danger of "death" (death in terms of heaven). Hence, all the healings that Jesus goes about doing -- as an example! For if we love our enemies, offer our gifts, heal whomever we can - then, in time, our own lives (that of the One Body) wil be healed - and what does that look like? It looks like heaven.

(an image I would like to explore further! - What does a world after our collective action to do the Moral Teachings of Jesus look like? If we were/are all to do this - What on Earth would that look like!?)

And here is the precept from Jesus to focus on today - and let tomorrow take care of tomorrow.

"Do not worry about tomorrow; tomorrow will take care of itself. Sufficient for a day is its own..."

Matthew 6:34

So, maybe for practice this week (without making "an oath") I could try really observing my practice exercise of The Golden Rule - and when in doubt of how to do - peace into action. I should meditate on what I've explored here today, this morning. And here! - we are provided further guidance! ? our words! to speak our truths - to let our ears hear and our hearts to listen! Then to speak from our hearts! So, if I am feeling that my gifts are not being well-accepted - I should seek to understand - in a way that The Golden Rule prescribes - so that others might hear as we ourselves would want to hear.

If "the lamp of the body is the eye" (Matthew 6:22) and "things that come out of the mouth come from the heart" Matthew 15:18, then it stands to reason that we should purify that which we see as well as that which is in our hearts.

SECOND WEEK (contemplations)

Cycle 3

The use (and purpose) of Parables. Understanding with your heart - see with eyes, hear with ears, the carpenter's son, "Where did this man get all this?"... looking up to heaven, he said the blessing, broke the loaves, and gave them to his disciples..." "went up on the mountain by himself to pray" " Take courage, it is I," "... that they might touch only the tassel on his cloak... [and]... healed." "the things that come out of the mouth come from the heart." "gave thanks, broke the loaves, and gave them to the disciples." "Rise, and do not be afraid." "Whoever humbles himself like this child is the greatest in the kingdom of heaven." "Therefore, what God has joined together, no human being must separate." "Let the children come to me, and do not prevent them; for the kingdom of heaven belongs to such as these." "the Son of Man did not come to be served, but to serve and give his life.".... "Amen, I say to you, if you have faith and do not waver... whatever you ask for in your prayer with faith, you will receive." ☐# The Greatest Commandment "You shall love the Lord, your God, with all your heart, with all your soul, and with all your mind... The second is... you shall love your neighbor as yourself."

Matthew chapter 13

Speaking in Parables, the measures of things, the foundation of "the" world, sharing of the loaves and "fishes," touching the tassel of a healer's cloak, great faith, "the things that come from the mouth, come from the heart."

The use of Leaven - being aware from whom & with what you "leaven" your life.

What does it mean "whatever you bind on earth shall be bound in heaven, and whatever you loose on earth, shall be loosed in heaven" - what does that mean? 17:7 "Rise, and do not be afraid." 18:4 "whoever humbles himself like this child is the greatest in the kingdom of heaven," 18:20 "For where two or three are gathered in my name, there I am in the midst of them." 19:6 "Therefore, what God has joined together, no human being must separate." 19:14 "let the children come to me, and do not prevent them, for the kingdom of heaven belongs to such as these." Matthew 20:16 > "Thus, the last will be first, and the first will be last."

the cleansing of the Temple. 21:21-22... "Amen, I say to you if you have faith and do not waver... whatever you ask for in prayer with faith, you will receive." Be reverent & appreciative of hospitality. The Greatest Commandment 22:37 "'You shall love the Lord, your God, with all your heart, with all your soul, and with all your mind.' - [and] 'You shall love your neighbor as yourself.'" 23:19 "which is greater, the gift, or the altar which makes the gift sacred?'" mint, dill, cummin 23:38 "'But the one who perservers to the end will be saved.'" 24:31 "'and he will send out his angels with a trumpet blast, and they will gather his elect from the four winds, from one end of the heavens to the other."

Some moral lessons: treasure both old wisdom and be refreshed by new wisdom; take time to sift through that wisdom borne from a practical place and that wisdom passed down through the ages. Share your food and nourishment will become bountiful and abundant. Have faith; believe - pray with faith, be sure my prayers match up to what is in my heart. Purify my heart first, like a temple - for words, prayers, and life flows from the unspoken intentions of the heart. Forgive so that my heart is full of nothing but light. Always give thanks upon reception of food and before breaking into it. What does it mean (in 16:24) to "take up (your) cross, and follow (him)" - What does that mean? And then it goes on to say "[we will be] repay[-ed] everyone according to his conduct?" This time is vastly and tremendously important: <u>trying</u> to reflect on the Moral Teachings of Jesus with particular emphasis on God's Love within Our Humanity," but my spirit isn't always truly in it. Sometimes, I keep looking at the clock; my mind keeps wandering; my head is not diving into the waters - I feel like this <u>day</u> could slip away into meaning-less ness unless I go <u>DO</u> something! out in the world; beyond this neighborhood, beyond my known family (into which I happened to have been born). I wonder what <u>did</u> Jesus <u>do</u> on <u>his</u> Birthday? Was that the 'one' day he took off and went atop the mountain to pray and be solely with God? What did he <u>eat</u> on his Birthday? Did he have a special feast? Did he invite anyone? Whom did he invite? What time must we rise and set to have each day have lasting-memory-potential. Sometimes, I feel upset with God, myself, for the dreams I had or did not have the ability to savor and understand. What shall we do when our hearts haven't clicked into place. Should we let go, many times we've just cried, because life can be so dysfunctional at a level that is deceptive. On some days we feel more heartache and suffering. This can be a blessing if we allow ourselves to experience it without getting dragged into its grasp. Sometimes, I think "I don't know that I've motivated <u>anyone</u> to be a better person today or create true & genuine happiness or that I've inspired anyone to do something great that will help us, as a culture, become kinder, gentler, warmer, courteous, compassionate, loving... I just don't feel that I've made that level of difference. I may be craving true leadership, to truly change our culture to be good, kind, loving, peaceful" - but , we can continuously ask, "how might I <u>do</u> that: if I don't feel that way in my Heart?!?" Maybe I do, though, maybe I do. Maybe there IS

more than meets the mind.

In fact, we <u>will</u>!!! Oh Dear Lord God, - it is through our adoration and trust in you that we find the will and the way. Thank you for wisdom, love, wholesome people, good friends, good companies, {list of specific companies and co-workers}

I have hope. I truly do. I believe, I do. And I'd really <u>like</u> to "Rise, and ... not be afraid." but I am. I do feel afraid. I've experienced real misfortune. I've been heart-broken. "Dear Lord God," I must pray, "I need the influence of the Holy Spirit to let my Light Shine."

177

THIRD WEEK
(contemplations)

Cycle 1

In the gospels there is a lot of time spent on "Healing" -- these are usually in the form of either healing the body or healing the spirit. The healing of the body shows the physical change - and likely appears more miraculous to witnesses. These take the form of healing the blind, the deaf, lepers, physical deformities, chronic illness, and even death. There are a similar amount of examples of removing evil spirits from people, and freeing people of this sort of oppression. Here the teaching objectives of Jesus seem to be to "have faith" and to "express gratitude." It is those with faith that were healed - even if they were far from his presence. It seemed to be always "your faith has healed you." The gospels are comprised of lots and lots of examples of healing.

Do I know where I am broken?

Do I know where I am sick?

Do I know what I cannot see? or cannot hear?

Do I know what demons my body & spirit host?

What is faith? What are we to have faith in?

In God? In Jesus? I don't see evidence to suggest one another, but maybe so - and maybe that is part of the role of the disciples - "ordinary" men and women who were to go out with only 1 tunic and one pair of sandals; and a walking stick but no food, no sack, and no money in their belts. In a way, doing so (and having instructed them to do so) was almost like Jesus saying to them "have faith in your fellow man." In every town, there was to be at least one hospitable person or family. And to go only as you are and with no victuals [for the future] is to go with great faith: faith in God and the Holy Spirit to provide, and faith in humanity to be generous and hospitable. What they did carry were invisible parcels. This is why the

"Parable of the Lamp" is so interesting. It is the Light they carried from within that shone forth; providing the way to open before them. I like the "Parable of the Lamp."

Hers is Mark's version:

He said to them, "Is a lamp brought to be placed under a bushel basket or under a bed, and not to be placed on a lampstand? For there is nothing hidden except to be made visible; nothing is secret except to come to light. Anyone who has ears to ear ought to hear."

He also told them,

"Take care what you hear. The measure by which you measure will be measured out to you, and still more will be given to you. To one who has, more will be given..."

What I like is this sense that the lamp burns within side of each of us. We carry that lamp wherever we go; and its light is not hidden - whether dim or bright, whether soft or harsh; its glow will be made known.

I also like this parable because of sentimental reasons; it harkens back to when I was at Peachtree Road United Methodist Preschool; we sung "This Little Light of Mine," and I remember singing it with all the air in my lungs, and I was already sure that I wanted to be a light in God's eye; and I found the words soon to say, in secret - my heart's desire.

And we sang, "this little light of mine, I'm gonna let it shine; this little light of mine, I'm gonna let it shine; let it shine; let it shine; let it shine." And I remember singing it, and I sang with all my breath; the breath from within every dendrite of my lungs and from the soles of my feet and the tips of my toes. I sang out those words once I had learned them, all of my body became filled with the breath of that song. And so, even today, decades later, I remember wisdom taught early in my childhood through song -- to be a light, and to let my let shine.

It is evident that we are here to practice faith.

The elders, the scribes, the Pharisees - are not lauded; they are not highly praised or admired or upheld as true exemplars. It is anybody who has faith - whether or not their past profession is savory or not. Whether or not they were of a certain class or ethnicity or culture or race or religion or socio-economic background. The true exemplars come from unexpected backgrounds, they can be anybody! They are us. The Good Samaritan, Mary Magdalene, the earliest disciples and Apostles, the outcasts, Saul, who became Paul,... those who were willing to turn a corner at a cross-roads and do good by their choices in this one wild and precious life.

From a small seed, grows a mighty plant.

From the sea, a storm is calmed.

From 5 loaves & 2 "fishes" come food for five thousand men and 12 wicker baskets full.

From 7 loaves & a few fish come food for four-thousand and 7 baskets.

"Your faith has saved you; go in peace" Jesus says again Luke 7:50, and again

There is the "simile of Light" (Luke 11:33) in addition to the Parable of the Lamp. and the call for courage especially when facing 'persecution' - what does all this have to do with "Moral Teachings?!?"

I'm not sure yet; I'm just writing as things come to me. There are times of great abundance in which we see dif-ferently, when we have felt the wealth, value, care, and ability to be generous that we had earned/ gained. We offer bottles of wine, baguettes, delicious chocolate when we meet with friends; we try to be more gracious and fair. We honor our relationships and pay back our debtors -- we shop with local mer-chants and at farmers' markets; we take on greater portions of the cost of living; and we think, with gratitude, how won-derful it is to experience abundance, what it feels like to meet all our needs and be generous.

But all-in-all; those times are not the full breadth of life, and we are grateful that we have tasted breakthroughs and glimpses of the other side. Compassion demands much of our Journey.

What does this have to do with these Moral Teachings?

Well, only that I know that we have the capacity to thrive. I have tasted fresh-ly-caught salmon & capers; I have eaten raspberries directly off the plant. I have tasted accomplishment. I have learned to swim in many waters. I have seen some light, but not all and not for long.

What does all this have to do with the Moral Teachings?

I ask again.

Well, it must be something my Heart is trying to rediscover, --

Faith (in God & fellow); gratitude; & my Light.

What theme do you sense?

Moral Teachings will emerge from all these rambling reflections >>

Have faith.

Demonstrate gratitude.

Cultivate the Light within our body & soul.

And then "go and do likewise."

The Parable of the Good Samaritan is ever-present, and I acknowledge its wisdom here, now.

"Take care of him. If you spend more than what I have given you (two silver coins), I will repay you on my way back."

This is something! This says a lot; no wonder its references are many.

A "traveler came upon a [beaten half-dead man] and was moved with com-passion -- he poured oil and wine over his wounds and bandaged them. Then he lifted him up onto his own animal, took him to an inn, and cared for him."

I could easily speculate about "Why?" But then I may miss the Moral Teaching

- which is to let ourselves be moved with compassion, to let ourselves stop during our travels and take the time and resources to care for someone, to let ourselves be generous with our resources to help bring life back to our fellow companions on this road of life.

The gospels do not continue with the story and say what became of the traveler, the beaten man, or the innkeeper. It mentions nothing of the traveler even being repaid -- it mentions nothing about expectations or revitalization. >>

What it does - is exhibit an example of being "moved with compassion."

I can't help but wonder who is a Levite and who is a Samaritan, and "why" that is important to this parable - and yet I feel like it could be a "scholarly distraction."

THIRD WEEK (contemplations)

Cycle 2

The Emotions of beings are a fascinating study for this context. Men (males) do not (or may be less aware) that they are subject to hormone-influenced moods and emotions. Women (within some age range, perhaps, or not) are more aware of the interplay among hormones, moods, attitude, perspective, and emotions. These things are more related to others. Whatever the causation of emotions, it is helpful to be compassionate with them - they are fascinating catalysts for furthering energy of various sorts. What does this have to do with "moral teachings [of Jesus]," "God's Love" or/and "Our Humanity" -- ? Well, I don't know yet - I'm writing to discover. During some times, we may sense some mild hallucinations on the wings of our awareness. We may "feel" (sensory perception of skin) more than 'normal,' too. We might quite respond differently to and participate in the world than "the other day." Our chemistry and circumstances are constantly changing, but there is always hope to
from a world on generic stability or usually

times, this is simply a result of the food we have eaten or our chemical surroundings (ie. air we breathe, beverages we drink, and all other consumptions). This can go high, and it can also provide additional challenges when our "health and well-being" is less-than-optimal.

On these peculiar days - we may need moral instruction, more directly and explicitly, in order to do well by our fellow beings - as much as we may need to be the recipient of moral behavior - we may need more expressions of love on these days. We may need more kindness preferred us. We may need more tenderness. We may need not-to-be-judged. We may need not to be left alone- but to be shown care without over-involvement. It's not that we even feel more introverted, it's just that we feel more affected by interaction. So, each interaction, exchange,... means more... in a way, for comparison and analogy - the "exchange rate" is higher - or perhaps, in a manner of speaking, the 'price of gold' goes up - or something to that effect. Basically, we may be less apt to let the water flow off our backs.

... here's the point: some days we simply feel more; we are more sensitive - both physically and emotionally. When we are beginning to understand, we are also beginning to see more: The preciousness of time. Especially as milestone days approach and we become aware of how physical presence and physical exchange affects so much of our emotions. When we are particularly affected , in [emotional] awareness, by what our body is doing, we can also be quite "high" during this time, too, because of the intensity of awareness.

Whichever emotion rests within me - it seems to become intensified and it lingers longer - causing me to consider it, note it, see it. How do the Moral Teachings of Jesus instruct us during these times? Well,... to be understood - these times are different than the death of a loved one - because that affects a group in a relatively similar time frame = or a holiday singular time's, which also affects groups rather observatively

180

are hidden (for the most part, usually) and not in the "same schedule" as every being at the same moment in society, community, culture - in truth, I find it fascinating and weird - and I wonder what governs the timing? Water, the gravitational effects of the sun, moon, earth... the closeness of other magnitudinous bodies (including loved ones and life!) The mysteries of life are throughout everything.

Proverbs tells of the "moral benefits of wisdom" and I wonder about Jesus' teachings. Perhaps, wisdom, as such, can be gathered from the manner with which Jesus approaches "the Sick" - although to compare natural cyclical chemical fluctuations within our bodies and minds to 'sickness' feels wrong. It is to me, is more like pen-ultimate health! so this becomes an even more fascinating dive into the Moral Teaching of Jesus.

And something additional: what of "cleanliness?"...

Surely it is of utmost importance for each of us to tend towards ourselves always as a physical temple - to keep our bodies clean, to smell clean, to anoint (with simplicity and humility and graciousness), to also take care of what we put into our bodies - for we are sensitive, each and all, to these things -- they make up our chemistry, indeed!

And there may be parallels to "fasting" - for in a way I fast from physical stimuli - I fast from moving about among too many others. I want only to connect to that which is most sacred, divine, heartening, true - and fills me with Light. I do feel joy, resonance, connectivity, happiness, warmth, sensations - it's just that I feel it more intensely - and I want to connect to my Treasure (those of the soul) and not just the every-moving swirl of life. I want to connect specifically and at-length to love, to magic, to miracles, to good tastes and smells. I want to drink deeply. - for my throat, of my nose, from my ears - my whole being.

And, I sometimes say, "It all seems to matter NOW."

Therefore, we must go with the flow; recognize the flow; let go of judgement; let go of control. Dance with life - not box people out or box people in -or shut down or shut off - or obsess over details - especially in the eyes of others. We must not go overboard, overcompensate, or overlook who we really are.

it is like the lessons I learned from Permaculture with actual life experience; the true nature of vectors must be accounted for, recognized, and yes even honored - perhaps it is not them that need to change my environment or the fertility in the soil surrounding its roots (like the parable of the fig tree in the garden that was not producing). I must approach each moment as the MOST REAL BLESSING. Each moment is of its own - and there are SO many vectors at interplay in the universe of innumerable worlds that I play only a fool to think I can control enough of them to have expectations met exactly as I dream them on "envision" them - This is why Jesus instructs us in the ways of Prayer!

"Ask, Seek, Knock" - God knows. God knows!

So what shall I do in the place of worry, in the place of judgment,...?

I shall shine my Light. If I could even just do this ONE thing very well - then my Life will bless me, I do believe. If I embrace Matthew 5:14 "You are the light of the world-"

At each moment, each REAL AND PRESENT MOMENT, all I need to do - is - be my Light.

Wow! What a challenge!! What a glorious challenge!

The "don'ts" are more easily visible; therefore, I want to understand the do's. Do let my light shine..., do love my enemies, do pray for those that persecute me, do ask, seek, knock; do... stretch out my hand....

THIRD WEEK (contemplations)

Cycle 3

I'm going to let <u>myself</u> feel my way through this one - just as I feel with as little pretense as I can. ... I've loved in many ways that exalt me; I don't understand it. I've loved <u>so</u> much, <u>so</u> deeply, <u>so</u> thoroughly. And likely continue to love those whom I've most sincerely loved until that very moment that I pass beyond the veil. There's some "odd" connection I have with angels on earth that has moved me from the realm of my dreams to my waking life. I can't explain it. It's like an intimacy of the soul, and it can be confusing. I'm an open, honest, authentic person, but this conundrum <u>baffles</u> me. I don't understand; I hunger for understanding. I thirst for it. Because otherwise, the perspective seems to click into place rather well. I'm a loving-person. I love deeply and soulfully, the gate will remain open. It's true for my sister. It's true for my brothers. It's true for every friend I've ever been fortunate enough to have. I feel like I shouldn't let myself get to hung up on it. But, periodically, I do, primarily because I <u>DO</u> care about healthy relationships. They are like <u>the</u> most important things to me. How shall we maintain the healthiest of relationships? When my dearly-beloveds actually <u>appear</u> to be suffering, why does my perception of the other person's suffering seem to be what hurts me more than the challenges that I directly face? I don't want those I love to suffer! I don't. I want them to thrive - even if it must be at the cost of our time together. I <u>Believe</u> in the Power of Love. I <u>Believe</u> in its MAGIC! I truly believe that the kind of love I feel when I resonate with the Holy Spirit can heal <u>all</u> wounds, all suffering - and can make this world whole & healthy, especially if we are all together on this mission. So, I continuously ask for guidance along this path; to be shown the way, to be given the strength, and the fortitude, and the Vision to see. I <u>want</u> to do good work. I am hungry to be taught how to Love with <u>great</u> Love, through <u>great</u> Heart in the way that is so radically healthy that it heals all things, all people, all relationships through which I breathe

my Life. These are my deepest, pureset desires. I hope that we shall not make too many mistakes along this path of your Greatest Gift of Love, especially that of failing to try to connect to the Divine Spark throughout us all.

I trust you, God; I believe in you. I believe in this path."Have I learned sufficiently?" I wonder. Well, I do think so. The way I treated my friend "yesterday" and the way I treated (responded to) my brothers and sister is showing me that I've matured, and maturing is an effect of learning. And perhaps we're never complete maturing. I really <u>DO</u> believe in True Love.

"If not 'now,' when?" "and if not 'when,' how?" I don't even know what I mean by that. I'm just trying to open my mind each day and night and <u>learn</u>. Deeply learn and thoroughly see. Yes, indeed - and to understand; and to end suffering - suffering for myself, suffering for anyone I have loved, suffering for all the inhabitants of this planet.

Except that I am lazy, Lethargic, and too-often lack clarity. I am highly flawed.

I'm not even a "motivated thinker." I give up. I quit. I pause. I don't complete things. I leave things up in the air. I don't follow through - as one basketball trainer-coach said to me in highschool, I make million-dollar moves and then nickel-shots. I lettered as a Freshman; but I didn't embrace the Pride. For whatever reason or combination of reasons; I let a Fear of success stifle me. Oh Dear Lord - how many of your People Live in Fear? A Fear; Fears more crippling than mine?

Oh my Dear Lord God - can we Heal the Earth's inhabitants in this one Generation's Lifetime? Please. Guide me. I AM a Believer. but I just want to BE. I don't want to "work so hard" - I want my <u>Life</u> to be my work, and my work to be valued, appreciated, Loved, revered, followed as an example. Lord God, I want you to Guide me so that <u>I</u> can be a leader. So that I will Be the leader that you've 'always' cultivated me to be. I am a leader. We are each leaders. I am a Lover. We are each lovers in this life. I <u>am</u> a Peace-maker. We each seek peace. I don't need to try hard. This work is <u>not</u> difficult. It is easy. And the easiest thing to DO should be being true to ourselves. Please Guide me to that Flow. Please Guide me with the Holy Spirit - always <u>always</u> inflame my Heart and the Vision through which I perceive this world. Lord God, I embrace the role of BEing your disciple, but if so; if that's what you truly ask of me. Then, please Guide me always. every moment, every interaction - and from <u>now</u> on, please help me to naturally, effortlessly, easily eradicate all suffering that passes through my life. Surely <u>that</u> is Possible! And if not, then to breathe through it and trust; for surely healing; a deeper healing is in the works.

Where am I motivated? Where am I inspired? Where do I feel energized? Yes, Dear Lord God - in adoration of you - through my Loves. Our love - making blessed by you. All night in your name. throughout the day, in your name. All of our BEing and actions in your name. Our choices blessed by you. I don't even know how, God - but I believe. I have to believe. And maybe floundering through difficulties was a Blessing; maybe there's a better spacetime for our conventions. Maybe --- maybe there are dreams that await me - and it's time to go to sleep and succumb to them; as it is to succumb to my Life. (whatever that is --) Oh; Dear God, Heavenly Father; I adore you. I adore you, <u>so</u> Greatly. I hope I Praise you with my Life. Guide me. Teach me. Lead me. Through <u>every-thing</u> I do, through all my choices -even faltering & lazy, I adore you. Thank you.

FOURTH WEEK (contemplations)

Cycle 1

There is hurt. There are difficulties. There are periods of darkness and pain. Those whom I love most deeply I invest the truth in - my truth; for that is really all I can say or write or share - if I am articulate enough; if it is a good day and it is a day where I am endowed with good articulation during tumultuous times. What is Life? What Life did God intend for us, collectively? What life did God intend for each of us, individually? What of my Life? I pause here to think and breathe through these questions that I have written, making sure that they are mine and not those of some wayward media. Lord God, Heavenly God, Almighty Father -- please enlighten me. Illuminate the Way of Love for me.

I have come to believe that such a way is navigated by communication. I have come to believe it is found through truth and sharing that which we each know to be true and hold as true. For Jesus spoke, "I am the Way, the Truth, and the Light." So, why am I feeling that twisted, knotted, mixed-up topsy-turvy sensation when trying to navigate how to deal with my relationship to/with [other]? -- this analogy of "friction" conjures images of hundreds upon thousands of years of conflict in the Middle East - the holiest of places; the Mecca, the hearts & cradles of the Judeo-Christian-Islamic traditions. I tried asking, " What would Jesus do?" but here I am, at home among my own brothers and sister, my own mother and father, all of our kin, all of our direct relations.

Today, now - with this knotty mixed-up problem.

But there is no discussion of his siblings and their relationships. He mentions "my brothers and sisters," but I do not know how they navigated such dynamics and "growing pains" - "What would Mary do?" Is the 2nd question I asked.

And then I began to feel the light, the spark of wisdom - her Love; a mother's love, a woman without sin. She had a sister. Yes, indeed, she did. I can turn to Mary, and so I did. I prayed -

"Hail Mary, Full of Grace, the Lord is with thee.

Blessed art thou among women, and blessed is

the fruit of thy womb, Jesus.

Holy Mary, Mother of God, pray for our sinners

now and at the hour or our death." Amen -

And then I arrived at a way forward.

I have had opportunities to focus on the Moral Teachings of Jesus with particular emphasis on God's love within our Humanity.

Throughout each past Lent we often revisit the weight we've carried of all matter, and how heavy such can be in our heart -

But "love is a force more powerful than gravity"

Listen, listen to the other's perspective.

Listen to their truths. Listen to their story.

Listen to their needs.

How might I express my "deep care" for our relationship and for each individual; in a way that feels loving? What should I REALLY do? Beyond these pages; beyond these thoughts; beyond this conversation with "Spirit" (God, Jesus, Mary "et al") What should I ACTUALLY DO? Beyond this desk; this "lamplight;" the quiet of the night -- what is Right?

Then, I challenge myself. I wonder, "do I REALLY care this much? Why should I care for others?

Then, I do "What ifs" - What if I ... x? What if I ... y? What if I ... t?

I should have confidence in the truth, I feel. I should have confidence in the way of love - when I communicate from a place of love, a place of learning, a place of shared understanding, a place of compassion all seems to flow quite well, quite well indeed.

So, Jesus, throughout your Moral Teachings, what wisdom do you have for me on "conflict resolution?" In my mind I hear you say, 'talk it out.' hmm,

There are emotions between two people; there are other stories that may enter into the minds that may not be relevant to growth by enduring once more. Then, there becomes increasing dynamics. And others, close ones, get pulled in - the force of Gravity acts and the bodies closest... well, Jesus didn't teach me this - not yet, as I see it.

Lord God, Heavenly God, father of all creation [including the owl who hoots outside my window] -- teach me the way through this, bring us into growth and healing. I would like to do this well, to navigate this path of relationship-building and healing as a testimony to your Guidance, with Grace and your wisdom and the Holy Spirit [brightly aflame] in my Heart.

What is the way forward? What is the way?

How might I act as your disciple and not as a sinner, tainted by the influence of evils? Let me do your will, Lord God - teach me; show me. How might I embody "God's Love within our Humanity?" At times, I have reacted too hastily with mis-perceptions; I should have acted more in line with the Moral Teachings of Jesus. This is a good time to practice.

FOURTH WEEK (contemplations)

Cycle 2

Matthew 16:26, as seen on sign while walking towards Grant Park:

"What good will it be for a man if he gains the whole world, yet forfeits his soul?"

In other words, "What can a man give in exchange for his soul?"

This was spoken in the passage wherein "Jesus Predicts his Death."

What meaning does this verse have for our lives? for how we show up in every moment? for how we show up to our work at hand? for how we show up to our relationships? to how we speak and thus -forth- honor our spoken words?

Listening concurrently to Jesus Christ Superstar while writing throughout Lent can be both powerful and inspirational, but it can also distract from the depth of the task at-hand.

Reading about "the greatness of Mordecai," I was offered a different perspective in appreciating the stories of Jesus being a Jew, himself.

"'It is written: +Man does not live on bread alone.+'"

Luke 4:4 and "'It is written: Worship the Lord your God and serve him only.'" Luke 4:5

The challenge within our Humanity is to know Who God Is. God is the same & universal, yet God may be accessible in different ways to different people in different bioregions. How do we come to know Who God Is? And so I ask, "Who is God?" "How do I know I'm serving 'him only?'" "What are the indicators that I am honoring and adoring 'God' and not something or someone else?" This is a very tricky concept. And so my interpretations become my beliefs. And then my beliefs become the foundation from which I act. If only I could recall information easily - how many times did I study and teach "The Iceberg Model (a tool for guiding Systems Thinking)," but I can't remember it exactly. Something like this:

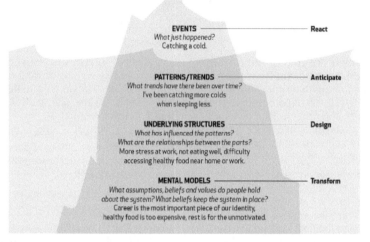

THE ICEBERG
A Tool for Guiding Systemic Thinking

EVENTS — **React**
What just happened?
Catching a cold.

PATTERNS/TRENDS — **Anticipate**
What trends have there been over time?
I've been catching more colds
when sleeping less.

UNDERLYING STRUCTURES — **Design**
What has influenced the patterns?
What are the relationships between the parts?
More stress at work, not eating well, difficulty
accessing healthy food near home or work.

MENTAL MODELS — **Transform**
What assumptions, beliefs and values do people hold
about the system? What beliefs keep the system in place?
Career is the most important piece of our identity,
healthy food is too expensive, rest is for the unmotivated.

No company is God. No college or university of academic institution is God. Systems Thinking is not God. Google is not God. The Grateful Dead is not God. Nature is not God. Music is not God. My best and most beloved friends are not God. God moves through all these things - organizations of atoms and particles and energy and people and light and… It's like the ebb and flow of all matter and energy. It is close to Nature and close to Music.

Does Jesus tell us who God is? Does Jesus instruct us on how we will recognize God?

(a) Who is God? It is something I'd like to learn more about, but for these Lenten exercises, the objective is to focus on the moral teachings of Jesus with particular emphasis on God's love within our Humanity.

I am curious about all the passages that allude to the Hebrew texts - to which Jesus quotes or references. Does he emphasize them and say they were "right" ways of conduit or does he de-emphasize them and ask for us to challenge their "rightness?"

So, then the questions become different? How do we protect ourselves from thieves, from evil-doers, from threats… and, perhaps Jesus answers this, too - "love your enemies," "do not worry," Why are people "thieves" - do they not have enough, are the wanton for something, do they have a deep oppressive-founded fear of speaking out for their needs, afraid to ask for help, a feeling of incapability to provide for one's needs and desires, is it pride? How might thieves reconcile with the past? What of "honest thieves?"

Honest thieves, dishonest thieves, evil-doers -- those after power, those after the control of wealth, those who enslave others and "bend others' wills" to serve their own. The simple answer would be to "kill them" - but that is not the "right answer" - But God does not bend. (?) God is almighty. (?) Isn't it better to recognize the good inside - and then for us to pile upon our resources to bring them back into their own light?? how? By speaking with truth. IF we speak the truth (our truth, our perception) to all and equally - then we do not give up our own power - and learnings, they gather great light.

FOURTH WEEK (contemplations)

Cycle 3

186

Matthew 7: Stop judging, that you may not be judged. For as you judge, so will you be judged, and the measure with which you measure will be measured out to you … remove the wooden beam from my eye first."

What constitutes "the wooden beam" in my eye (that is not all the splinters in my relations' eyes).

"Ask and it will be given to you; seek and you will find; knock and the door will be opened to you. For everyone who asks, receives And the one who seeks, finds; and to the one who knocks, the door will be opened."

Know how to give good gifts to your children.

Do to others whatever you would have them do to you.

It is difficult for me to focus on the Psalms because they are so obsessed with the language of war. I have no interest in war. I'm interested solely in the ways of Joy and in Peace. I am interested in Love. I am interested in love. I am interested in Heaven. I am interested in Light. It is difficult for me to focus on the Gospels because they are written for men, and I am not a man. I am a woman. I am feminine. It is a different energy, a different "Force," a different [sense of] "Power." Fortunately, within Matthew 5 and a few chapters there is relevance. Things about Light and Treasures in Heaven and there's some guidance on how to mend relationships -, but how shall I apply all this? today; here now - with these things that feel the most complex and twisted and irreconcilable. What's the issue? What's the "sin" [against me]? What "resolution" am I looking for? Simply for my relations to be authentically kind and loving to me and our direct relations? Is it as simple as that? What does that even look like? What is the "sin" that we are committing? So I really and truly ask God for Guidance; I want to do the Right things, especially in regards to this. Even if it is difficult, I want to do the

Right Thing. Maybe I am.

{but in what ways have I acted similarly?} I wonder if "Proverbs" is a little more my flavor.

So, I pray.

And I don't have to "dance for 20 minutes" today because I'll be dancing like 5 hrs. at Brie's wedding reception party. I'm behind on reading the Psalms though, and I'm feeling the weight of the crosses I bear. I pray to the Lord God, though, and I trust in Him - and I'm preparing my Way - I know it's challenging work, but I REALLY want to live an exemplary life. I want to be a light of This Universe. I pray.

See it through completion, but follow the Guidance of Love - of God's Love; of Guidance on Being loving, being thoughtful, being kind - we've got these "struggles," But how am I supposed to deal with them? "Continue to be a living example of love," are the words I hear for all of us.

"Love is the only way."

FIFTH WEEK (contemplations)

Cycle 1

God, I took a figurative directive and literally applied it. What shall I do for this?

Or perhaps, what should I not do for this?

What were those times - from her perspective? from my perspective? Are they similar times?

Without being on the "moral high-ground"- and becoming like a "chief priest, an elder, or a scribe" - How <u>shall</u> I proceed?

God's love within our Humanity. Moral Teachings. -

What are the courses of the Way, the Truth, and the Light?

What shall we do?

What actions shall we take?

How shall we form our words?

Go up to the mountain and pray, if/ when needed.

Let seed fall on rich soil and produce fruit.

Do not be afraid; just have faith.

Let your heart be moved by compassion.

Feed the multitudes.

Wash one another's feet, especially your own followers/ those for whom you are their leader.

Pray the Lord's prayer : Our Father, Who art in Heaven, hallowed be thy name. ...

What of precepts?

Mark 11:23 > "Amen, I say to you, whoever says to this mountain, "Be lifted up and thrown into the sea; and does not doubt in his heart but believes that what he say will happen, it shall be done for him. Therefore, I tell you, all that you ask for in prayer, believe that you will receive it and it shall be yours.

When you stand to pray, forgive anyone against whom you have a grievance, so that your heavenly Father may in turn forgive your transgressions."

"Teach the way of God in accordance with the truth."

"You shall love the Lord your God with all your heart, with all your soul, with all your mind, and with all your strength."

AND, "you shall love your neighbor as yourself."

Moral imperatives? Moral direction? What questions do I have in retrospect of Lents past.

The Passover/ Seder has happened. So has the full moon of Lent and Easter. I have experienced "the future" that will have had occurred 20+ days out from when I should have written & reflected. At this time, in the past, I had spent 6 days in Durham with my sister-in-law, brother, nephew, and niece, and their cat. It was my best friend from childhood's 36th Birthday; the Vernal Equinox and all kinds of other astrological occurrences. I have had my own "significant" Birthday, and I felt love and loved. I felt caring and cared for. I felt grateful for my sister-in-law's friendship and my nephew's companionship. She opened a bottle of champagne. We toasted my brother. We toasted one another. In a manner-of-speaking, we toasted love & Blessings present. We acknowledged them, and in a way, I acknowledged the gift of my sister-in-law's friendship, her hospitality, her welcomeness, her generosity, the warmth of her spirit, her thoughtfulness -- during that week of my visit it was one of "the craziest" times of their life. My brother's job thing was solidified, the electricians came, demolition of their kitchen was beginning; other big projects/ accomplishments were coming to fruition - and yet they welcomed me wholeheartedly. They <u>let</u> me play with my nephew <u>all day</u>! And we created tremendously lovely memories together. They trusted me with their beloved son -- that trust, I felt. I feel blessed by it! Truly, I did & <u>do</u>.

This is to say a few things about what it feels like to live, actually live, with God's love in our hearts - to go forth and be thoughtful; to trust those who have earned trust. To welcome one another into our homes. To be hospitable, - and the guest is a blessing as well - as Jesus & his Disciples were when they traveled - only wearing a pair of sandals, no second tunic nor purse for food - that takes a lot of human faith!

"nothing for the journey but a walking stick - no food, no sack, no money in [our] belts!" but then he said to them 'Whenever you enter a house, stay there until you leave from there [that city]…" Thus, this style of traveling was also an example of the Mission of the Twelve.

"While they were eating, he took bread, said the blessing, broke it, and gave it to them, and said 'Take it, this is my body.' Then he took the cup, gave thanks, and gave it to them, and they all drank from it. He said to them, 'This is my blood of the covenant, which will be shed for many. … Then, after singing a hymn, they went out to the Mount of Olives."

There are several things that speak to me of "Moral Teachings" delivered by this passage in Mark 14:22;

One is the focus on Blessing bread and on giving thanks for a cup of drink, specifically wine.

A blessing and Thanks[giving].

They seem to be used almost interchangeably, but are they the same? Not really.

To bless our food (the bread) is to make it / deem it holy. What was Jesus' blessing? I wonder.

To give Thanks - is similar, but different - it is a direct expression of gratitude. I understand gratitude. I understand what giving thanks looks like, but what does a "blessing," as such really look like? Did Jesus exemplify that for us?

Also, I find it fascinating that the account takes the time effort and mentioned that "singing a hymn." I do

wonder what hymn they sang -- likely something from the Jewish faith & customs in relation to Passover; however & whatever it was, was not mentioned - is that because it was obvious -or- because it wasn't as important as the fact that the action of "singing a hymn" was undergone?

The fact that "singing" [at all] is part of the Gospels -- is of great interest to me, and fascinates me wonderfully!!

Then, there is the next path - going to the Mount of Olives. So, in summary - there are 4 key actions to tell us what Jesus did on the most important (last) meal of his life on earth -- !

Which no doubt would have been considered and intended to be celebrated with perfection.

He blessed the food. (bread).

He gave thanks for the cup (wine/ drink)

There was the singing of a hymn,

and they went out to the Mount of Olives.

These could be 4 guidelines for our own meals > and our own Last Wills and Testaments.

and what is now obvious to me; which wasn't before!! - is that Jesus supped with others on his final meal! He did not eat & drink "alone with God" - he ate & drank with his closest friends & loved ones, on earth, on earth!

He was with others. It says, "while they were eating." …

not while he was eating. It's not like he shut himself in a room to be contemplative - he celebrated! And he blessed the bread, gave thanks for the cup, sang a hymn, and then went out to the Mount of Olives -- fascinating!

FIFTH WEEK (contemplations)
Cycle 2

Sometimes, it is easy to love. Sometimes, it is difficult to love.

Consider real relationships & friendships throughout your life; the gifts of friendships, what is true? What is genuine? What feels like "Magic?" What feels blessed? What defines different types of relationships? partnerships?

What contributes to the healthiest of relationships?

What should 'dating' (even your spouse) flow like? and the union of Holy Matrimony?

What of the energy and intensity of 1:1 relationships?

How to nourish *all* one's many varieties of relationships?

List out all the relationships (in 3 columns: present, past, and potential; concrete and abstract) of your life? -- every manifestation and entity of consciousness. In what ways do you show up and be present?

How are you fulfilled in these relationships?

What fortunes do these relationships bestow upon your life?

What might be "missing?"

How might you be stretched?

Where can you show up with courage to engage socially, especially when you feel the compulsion to withdraw?

What do you value in your friendships?

How have you acknowledged them directly?

How can you allow God and the Holy Spirit to flow through your friendships and relationships?

How are all your relationships Blessings? Gifts?

How do your friendships and relationships fill you with wonderment and awe?

How do your friendships and relationships make your dreams come alive?

What does it feel like when you feel most-near to God?

In what ways do you listen to God?

What visions are a gift of the Holy Spirit?

How are you best able to live and communicate on earth with earthly being here and now and also maintain your connection to the Divine?

In what ways are you grounding into all eternity?

In what ways are you overflowing with love and adoration for God and such Blessings?

What makes it easy to find real wisdom that is applicable and that will "work" when you are most tried [emotionally]?

What does "works" or "wins" or "succeeds" look like [within the scope of the Moral Teachings of Jesus]?

Who / what can you reliably turn to for advice, especially when gnarly complex issues get escalated?

Who/ what do you Trust to influence your choice towards Wisdom and Righteousness with your specific set of circumstances?

Which spiritual texts help guide you along the Right Path?

Which of this wisdom is part of your Infinite Being?

What wisdom do you gather from within?

Where does the "wisdom from within" drink?

In what ways has the Good that you've striven for and achieved replenish your inner guidance; trust to choices?

What / who can you surround yourself with throughout your life to help fuel your Inner Guidance?

What good might you seek with every interaction? With every step? With every moment? Every decision? Every day; all the time?

In what ways do all the little details contribute to your [spiritual, emotional...] health & well-being?

In what ways can you navigate all of your life with, for God, in a way that nurtures deep unshakable trust in yourself?

In what ways can you cultivate your own internal wisdom?

In what ways can you nourish your body?

In what ways can you nourish your prized relationships?

In what ways can you live your life on high?

In what ways can you maintain healthy connections?

In what ways can you invite more "real" good things into your life?

In what ways are you giving the wisdom inside you permission to blossom, with God's Blessing? What invitations to participate in life's great wonders are you accepting?

In what ways does your presence and participation add value to others present?

In what ways do you <u>know</u>, <u>trust</u> that God has your heart in mind?

In what ways can you know and trust that God knows more than you about yourself as well as the external eternal dynamics of the universe?

In what ways are all your relationships worthy of God's attention?

What are your beliefs?

Do your beliefs make sense?

Do your beliefs fit in with the Moral Teachings of Jesus?

Do your beliefs resonate with your internal wisdom?

Do your beliefs create and nourish healthy relationships?

In what ways must you seek external guidance and ask for help?

In what ways must you "knock" at God's door?

Which of your relationships feel most important to receive help?

What dwells in your heart?

In what ways can you honor, respect the requests (Right Speech) of your relations?

In what ways can you act (speak) from a place of love, peace, health, well-being, respect, value...?

= GOD'S PROMISES for your every need =

"come singing into Zion" Isaiah 51:11

"Let not our heart be troubled; ye believe in God, believe also in me" John 14:1

"Peace, I leave with you, my peace I give unto you; not as the world giveth, give I unto you. Let not your heart be troubled, neither let it be afraid" John 14:27

"trust in the Lord with all thine heart; and lean not unto thine own understanding. In all ways acknowledge him, and he shall direct thy paths" Proverbs 3:5-6

FIFTH WEEK (contemplations)
Cycle 3

Be motivated and inspired by the good. Learn and cultivate the language of love and peace. Fully & wholly acknowledge the Miracles & Enchantment of each time. The awesome scenes of life! Those in which we witness ourselves wholly present. Those in which we are "in the zone" - when we have felt welcome and connected - and like you <u>really</u> wanted to study and improve upon your experiences. Consider those places in which you could connect and flow even more! Consider wherein respect flows easily and the abundance of Blessings are palpable. Note these.

On Good Friday, what a miraculous occasion it would be, regardless of upbringing, if that everyone within earshot and wavelength of each other stopped what they were doing between

12 & 3pm and prayed, meditated, and reflected -

If I adore God. If I love God - why is such a *brief* moment of silence, quiet, and peace difficult to do universally, to give it "for God." because - because of Life! I am living - I am working. I live outside an abbey. I do not live with the sacrament of Holy Orders - I live among the world-at-large. This is a conscious decision not to live a "cloistered life" - and in doing so - there are very much "trade offs" to what becomes of my time. There is a consistent stream of challenges. I'm a prayerful, contempla-tive, dreamer - an ambitious writer with minimalist ways - And I am grateful to God for all those Things which draw me out and Bless me. I want to feel what it's like to do the work the Holy Spirit has given me from a space that enlivens me. I want to allow good examples to infil-trate my life. Blessings of utmost grand-ness, I am so grateful. These hours make us all better, happier, more thoughtful, more connected, and raises us all above the daily troubles of mundane temporal drama - participating, and not aloof - but very much because of prayer, do we rise together in peace.

"Today" he suffered & died - he was placed in the tomb of Joseph of Ari-mathea. What a guy! Drinking, feasting, miracles - and then to die; to trust his Life to his father - that he would be ris-en; but during those hours he had only his Faith. And then he breathed his last breath as a man - he gave up his breath. He died. He experienced human pain, and then he died. Now, he is dead and the "veil of the sanctuary was torn in two from top to bottom" - and I always presumed it turned dark as night. Yes - it says so in Luke! Luke 23:44 "It was now about noon and darkness came over the whole land until three in the afternoon - because of an eclipse of the sun." ! - yes. I thought that's how I remembered it. Oh - and according to Matthew (27:45-46) Jesus "suffered" from noon - 3; and died at 3 o'clock. So he must've endured horribly for those three hrs. Like the worst of all endurances. All of Pain, of all

the Earth; assuming all of our suffering onto and into himself.

Did Jesus drink the wine from the Reed after he had called out to Elijah? The centurion is an interesting character to me, and so is Joseph of Arimathea. Jesus was taken down in the evening when his body was placed in the area of Joseph (not his father). Why him? Why his tomb? Fascinating.

I feel chilled right now; a breeze is blowing through this front window - it feels good. It is silent enough for an "International city" - I guess I miss the Atlanta before "Atlanta" was "Inter-national" - before it was a "big city" - when it still felt cozy & calm & lush with trees & creeks and places to explore. Where might I go & live with this Royal College of Inspiration. I could live "any-where" - I know I could. Dear Lord God, I pray. Thinking of Jesus and the gospels feels "Right," right now. I am grateful that I get to.

SIXTH WEEK
(contemplations)

Cycle 1

Miracles and awesomeness. That is God. God became man. How might I help to proliferate God's love within Our Humanity? Be "continually in the temple praising God" after the Ascension" [with great joy]." Great Joy, Luke says, "great joy." That is powerful. That is something: not "awe," not "fear," not "trembling," not "hope," not "trust," not "anticipation," not "yearning," nor "satisfaction," nor "comfort," not "assurance"... but "JOY!" - and not just "joy," but GREAT JOY. wow. That is something. Twice in that paragraph, Luke refers to the blessing Jesus gave the apostles [raised his hands and blessed them. As he blessed them he parted from them and was taken up to heaven]. Luke 23:50 ... and they "returned"... "with great joy,"... That is really something. They were not sad or curious or unsure... or maybe they were; such emotions are not mutually exclusive. But the fact remains that the word[s] chosen by "Luke" to express all of this was [great] joy. And that's how I strive to feel. I am striving to do good work, such that I might feel "great joy." I have felt joy; often times when completing a very difficult yet rewarding task. This is usually "work" - like reconciling the monthly bank statement or grading a bunch of papers or that sort of thing. -- or even from addressing a complex relationship problem with a truth that I have held in my mind.

But something about all this makes me feel like the "great joy" comes from something nearly imperceivable and inexplicable to [the common] man.

It's like -- here's God - Lord of all creation. He provides his only son.. His son is crucified, dies, resurrected and then ascends into Heaven -- these Disciples are witnesses in all of this. They are "incredulous for joy" they "were amazed" -- "he stood in their midst, and said to them 'Peace be with you." !!! I mean,

"wow!" Luke 23:36-53 does a pretty cool job of explaining all this.

I mean here they are - their Christ has been crucified & died - then he is resurrected; he stands in their midst and offers them peace by his words, "Peace be with you" -- he recognizes their humanity -- being "startled and terrified" - as if seeing a ghost. "Troubled" and with questions in their hearts.

He "became man" -- he understood the ways of man. For 32-33 years, he learned the ways of man -- the fear and the trembling - the rules that govern us; the suffering and struggling - the illnesses, sicknesses, death, and grief.

Why do we tremble -- the sight of Jesus resurrected should have been cause for rejoice, but it was not, at first, because it's terrifying - a man (Jesus) was dead for 3 days and then he rose, walked, stood, ate, and drink - as a man, once again.

Eventually they too overcame their fear - once they were "clothed with power from on high" -- and then they; after his Ascension, "returned ... with great joy."

According to Matthew the moral teachings of Jesus are those found in chapters 5-7 "The Sermon on the Mount" they are the Beatitudes; the similes of salt and light, Teaching about the Law, Teaching about anger, teaching about adultery and divorce, teaching about oaths, teaching about retaliation >

a call to the love of enemies, "teaching about almsgiving, teaching about Prayer, teaching about fasting, and our "treasure in Heaven" -- they are about the "Light of the Body," "God and Money," "Dependence on God," - "Judging Others" and throwing "Pearls before Swine." Jesus taught of "the answer to Prayers" -

"The Golden Rule" "The Narrow Gate" and then "false prophets," "the true disciple,"

And finally "the two foundations."

In all of this he provided "The Lord's Prayer" >

Our Father in heaven,
hallowed be your name,
your kingdom come,
your will be done,
on earth as in heaven.
Give us today our daily bread;
and forgive us our debts,
as we forgive our debtors;
and do not subject us to the final test,
but deliver us from the evil one.....

"Your Father knows what you need before you ask him." (Matthew 6:9)

and then in Matthew 7:7; we are provided some insight into how God, our Heavenly Father, will answer our prayers. It's just so amazing.!>

That all of this is (2020-~36=1987!) That it's all 1987 years old!!!!! (or so.)

That these stories have been told to billions of people. That billions have prayed "The Lord's Prayer!"

Billions have died since these words were written; these stories set down, the Messiah ascended into Heaven after being resurrected. That is just incredible! And we think Shakespeare is "the man" -- we think about Leonardo da Vinci or Martin Luther King -- or anyone; or any teachings - WHY have these persevered - is it about the sacraments (the "blood") is it something hidden from the canonized texts to which the Catholic Church KNOWS. The churches, the Cathedrals, the monasteries... ? The saints? There is something. Something in all this is Really Powerful: REAL Power.

And it feels, to me, like it is found in the words "Peace be with you" --

and ... "great joy,"...

It's interesting: for 4,000 years, God sent prophets, he "inspired" and "revealed," but then he chose to "become man" - why then? Why during the time of the Roman Empire, of Caesar?

Because of the expanse? a great marketing plan?? Because of "timing" --

Also, I'm interested in these "moral teachings" from the Sermon on the Mount:

Why those the most important teachings and are they still?

Yes "love of enemies" -- isn't that fascinating. And "judging others" - these precepts are fascinating and yes, very relevant. Question is: why is humanity prone to not loving our enemies and to casting judgment on others. Why do we habitually [in our culture] do these things. Why are we predisposed to hate our enemies and judge one another??

And why the "Beatitudes?" Why did I feel so compelled when I first learned of them as a child; so close to God; so one with the Holy Spirit? I felt the power of the Presence in my life. I felt alive with the soul. Alive with the spirit. Alive with wonder and awe and GOD! I felt blessed. I felt connected. I felt good and loving and kind and a child of God. I understood these messages, these moral teachings, I had a friend, and we were alive with wonder and creation! Invention and clubs and Life. I pray for a return of these such Blessings to all of us from the best of our childhood dreams. Amen.

SIXTH WEEK (contemplations)
Cycle 2
(pre-contemplations)

"He heareth the broken in heart, and bindeth up their wounds." Psalm 147:3

"For his anger endureth but a moment; in his favour is life: weeping may endure for a night, but joy cometh in the morning." Pslam 30:5

"Yea, though I walk through the valley of the shadow of death, I will fear no evil: for thou art with me, thy rod and thy staff they comfort me." Psalm 23:4

"Beloved, if our heart condemn us not, then, have we confidence toward God." 1 John 3:21

"Let not your heart be troubled: ye believe in God..." John 14:1

The Centurion's Mathew 8:8

"I will behave myself wisely in a perfect way. O when wilt thou come unto me? I will walk within my house with a perfect heart." Psalm 101:2

"Be strong and of a good courage, fear not, nor be afraid of them: for the Lord thy God, he it is that doth go with thee; he will not fail thee, nor forsake thee" Deuteronomy 31:6

"Let all bitterness, and wrath, and anger, and clamour, and evil speaking, be put away from you, with all malice; And be ye kind to another, tenderhearted, forgiven one another even as God... hath forgiven you." Ephesians 4:31-32

"And, behold, two of them went that same day to a village called Emmaus, which was from Jerusalem about three score furlongs. And they talked together of all these things which had happened. And it came to pass, that while they communed together and reasoned, Jesus drew himself near, and went with them." Luke 24:13-15

"We took sweet counsel together, and walked unto the house of God in company." Psalm 55:14

Benevolence

Luke 10:25

The Greatest Commandment

"There was a scholar of the law who stood up to test him and said, "Teacher, What must I do to inherit eternal life?" Jesus said to him, "What is written in the law? How do you read it?" He [the scholar] said in reply, "you shall love the Lord, your God, with all your heart, with all your being, with all your strength, and with all your mind, and your neighbor as yourself." He [Jesus] replied to him, 'You have answered correctly; do this and you will live."

>> then into the Parable of the Good Samaritan

But because he wished to justify himself, he said to Jesus, "And who is my neighbor?" Jesus replied, " A man fell victim to robbers as he went down from Jerusalem to Jericho. They stripped him and beat him and went off leaving him half-dead. A priest happened to be going down that road." ... and then it's the heart of the parable. the Samaritan traveler pouring oil and wine and bandaging his wounds... wow! cool works.

Luke is filled with practical observations of moral teachings.

Chapter 11 is good material - on the ways of prayer.

and the Simile of the Light in which we are reminded.

"The lamp of the body is your eye. When your eye is sound, then your whole body is filled." and "If your whole body is full of light, and no part of it is darkness, then it will be full of light as a lamp illuminating you with brightness."

Then, some hard truths in chapter 12 (2&3)

"There is nothing concealed that will not be revealed, nor secret that will not be known. Therefore whatever you have said in darkness will be heard in the light, and what you have whispered behind closed doors will be proclaimed on the housetops." This serves the GOOD we have, do, & say, too. So that the GOOD we've done will be made known even when it is not immediately acknowledged or lauded. This is like a reference to the kharmic flow of Things.

Luke 12:34 "For where your treasure is, there also will you heart be. "I love this passage. It feels like such a GIFT of Truth and Insight to me. Because what it is saying to me is this: that whatever I treasure will be like a magnetic force for my heart. And wherever my 'heart' is, that will be my sojourn through life, that will be my way - So if I treasure a letter from my niece, then my heart will be with her. If I treasure a memory, moment, or love for my nephew - then my heart will be there. If I treasure healthy friendships, then so too will my heart be with them and I will invest more of myself into them. If I treasure my home and my husband and our family, then we will be blessed by the good my heart will do toward those ends. If I treasure my relationship with God and with the Holy Spirit, then my heart will strive to please, and by pleasing it'll bring me closer to and into greater harmony with the reception of blessings by that treasure and the expression of my love and treasuring of that treasure.

Then in Luke 14:10 "Rather, when you are invited, go and take the lowest place so that when the host comes to you he may say, 'My friend, move up to a higher position.'

And The Parable of the Great Feast

And The Parable which demonstrates the way to ask for forgiveness - "Father, I have sinned against heaven and against you, I no longer deserve..."

Luke 15:21 - and this Parable of the Lost Son teaches us not only how to ask for forgiveness, but also how to grant it! And then in Luke 15:31 "'My son, you are here with me always, everything I have is yours, But now we must celebrate and rejoice because your brother was dead and has come to life again; he was lost and has been found.'" This is excellent! Here we are shown a glimpse of sibling-fueled jealousies - and we are shown how a wise, loving, and tender-hearted father (God, be blessed) would treat both and explain away the potential for harboring jealousy. It is really a grand Parable because it teach-

es so much about how to BE in a family. The anger by the older son seems totally justifiable - except we are instructed throughout these Moral Teachings not to succumb to anger. Jesus provides us an opportunity to visit an other perspective in the parable - which is marvelous.

I am interested in these moral teachings around our born sisters and brothers - the direct blood connection between siblings. It's such a weird thing - to be [presumed] so close, and yet many times of distant minds. It's a blessing and yet it occurs with such complexity.

The figurative "sisters and brothers" seems understandable to me - they are our "fellow man" - these are strangers, passersby, thieves, and even enemies - how to be loving to them seems easier to me - is it because that was one of the first lessons I learned from the gospels as a child? I remember learning that. I remember learning to "love thy enemies." It feels so complex to me - for one. Perhaps, the guidance here comes from Luke 17:33 "whoever seeks to preserve his life, will lose it, but whoever loses it will save it." And so in a way this is inviting us to let go of an attachment to outcome to let things flow as they will -- this is the parable that speaks of a trust beyond even the natural tendencies of humankind - to trust and walk towards God, with God and let go of that which is behind us. - to let go of the past; to walk towards the will of God with courage and peace of heart.

I am also quite good with the Moral Teachings as they refer to children - and Luke 18:!6 reminds me of the wisdom I kindle inside, "Jesus, however, called the children to himself and said, 'Let the children come to me and do not prevent them; for the kingdom of God belongs to such as these. Amen, I say to you, whoever does not accept the kingdom of God like a child will not enter it.'" The emphasis on our "children," "childhood," innocence, curiosity,... is of very much interest to me. The preparations for the Passover and the feast of Unleavened Bread is also fascinating to me. For Jesus was a Jew! And that fascinates me. That he was of a religious culture and he observed it, and did well & good by its customs.

I'd like to understand Jesus and his travels. He did a bit of traveling and teaching. He slept in different houses in different cities. He advised his disciples of a simple traveler's life, as well. But though he "traveled light," did Jesus have a home? Did he return with keep-sakes or oils or wines? - did he "own" *any*thing? ...

SIXTH WEEK (contemplations)

Cycle 3

"The Lord is my shepherd, I shall not want... he layeth me down in green fields."

Communication is <u>so</u> important. It is an energy - exchange though, and it requires the ingredient of time - but, honestly, not all <u>that</u> much time. Some communication can be 10-20 seconds or less than a minute! but it could save energy later and time - distribute later. Just enough words, with the right tones, at the right time - when they are sim-ple, direct, articulate - when they are thoughtful and genuine and sincere. Oh Dear Lord

SEVENTH WEEK (contemplations)

Cycle 1

Fascinating -- the turn of events. How space becomes filled with joy when allowed to be.

The suffering was difficult and complex. Then, in 3 days, Jesus Christ - the Messiah and Son of God - was risen! 'He is Risen! Alleluia' We sang and celebrated.

He was among the mortal world again for 40 days -

His very last 40 days on Earth (until he comes again) - Well, anyway, the point is that he returned after death to take the Moral Teachings that much further! that much deeper! from our humanity to our spirit! It's not just about how we do act - how should we go about life on Earth, but how do we open our hearts so that we might receive the Holy Spirit! So what's this all about?

Christ's teachings (for 3 years), then his suffering (humanity) and his death (mortality) - then his return (God's awesome power - even to 'conquer death') and then Peace - for Jesus returned saying "Peace be with you" -- and he returned saying "I have much more to say to you, more than you can now bear. But when he, the Spirit of truth, comes, he will guide you into all truth... In a little while you will see no more, and then after a little while you will see me."

.....''But you will receive power when the Holy Spirit comes on you.''... (Acts 1:8)

I have believed, in my life, that "power" is a product of evil, but why then would Jesus, the son of God, the Man - then wish to give his beloveds 'Power' (through the coming of the Holy Spirit). Lord God, I pray - that I may exercise the Power you give to me wisely, compassionately, and with Love. Oh My Dear Lord God, I adore you. Thank you!

And of Acts 2:1-13 when The Holy Spirit comes at Pentecost.

What it says is that they "were filled with the Holy Spirit and began to speak in other tongues, as the Spirit enabled them" - so it refers to the ability to speak - to speak truths in a way that allows for all people to connect and hear the teachings of Jesus, son of God.

This work of the Holy Spirit -- it does something; it transforms the messages. It transforms the messaging. It empowers believers to speak "on behalf" of Jesus's teachings. No longer is the New Testament dappled with red script. Jesus has ascended, and he (God) gave the Holy Spirit to Jesus' believers, even those that did not at first believe (Thomas) - and then entrusted those remaining of Humanity to teach one another.

Why should I then not trust my fellow mortals on this path through human life. God trusted men, not only his own son - but his "friends" -- he trusted them to carry out the teachings of Jesus, he trusted them to carry out the moral teachings.

I must learn to forgive.

I must learn to love - truly love, love

as one Spirit in God's creation.

I must learn to Trust.

I must learn to accept the spirit of God within me.

I must learn to respectfully & responsibly exercise the Power of the Spirit of God that has been given to me.

God, I adore you. Thank you.

Thank you for reminding me of your power.

Thank you for reminding me of you spirit.

Thank you for telling me / sharing with me that "where [my] treasure is, there [my] heart will be also." Thank you, Lord God, I adore thee.

SEVENTH WEEK (contemplations)

Cycle 2

John 3:1-10, John 7:50-51; John 19:39-42

Nicodemus, an influential member of the Sanhedrin. He and Joseph Arimathea - together asked Pilate if they could remove the body of Jesus from the cross on the Sabbath, Passover, and came bringing a mixture of myrrh and aloes - weighing about one-hundred pounds. And they took the body of Jesus and bound it with burial cloths along with the spices, according to Jewish preparation day; for the tomb was close by." This is fascinating! Who are these two men? What were their motives? Was it because they 'cared' for Jesus - or perhaps because they honored the Sabbath (Passover), their Judaism and their commitment to God. Whatever motivated them - I think was good. They did good. They were treating his body kindly and they buried him according to Jewish custom. This is important because it shows that even if they were simply cleaning and clearing the landscape for the Jewish people, they were still honoring that Jesus's heritage and a "good Jew" who deserved a proper Jewish burial. To me this says a lot! It is incredibly fascinating. ... Myrrh and aloes... and other spices; what are these? I understand why they are part of custom - so that the bodies decay without stench - why the aloes? Did they rub the aloes into his wounds to cover them? Those in his hands and feet where he was nailed to the cross? those on his back where he was lashed 39 times (why 39?), those on his forehead where the people placed a crown of thorns, that in his side where "on soldier thrust his lance... and blood and water flowed?" Did they (Nicodemus and Joseph of Arimathea) [em]balm those wounds with aloes? What did they do with the myrrh? And what of the other spices - ? And the burial clothes? Did they carry him from the cross and through the garden into the open tomb? Or did Pilate's men deliver the body? (what happened to the cross itself?) However, it happened, it seems to have been done with great care. And for whatever reasons it was done with such great care - fascinates me!

"Jesus suffered, died, and was buried."

This is what we proclaim in the Nicene Creed. This is our belief - the catechism of the Catholic faith.

Indeed it is evident on Good Friday that he suffered (or underwent pain, perhaps he did not "suffer" because he also practiced the Buddha's Teachings(?)) - that he was a man; that he was a man healthy of mind, body, spirit, and heart; he "suffered";" and then he died - and then he was buried -

And the gospels tell us about how he suffered and what the moments before his death were like. He was dead; there were witnesses. One soldier (at least), Pilate (likely), and then, of course, Nicodemus, and Joseph of Arimathea - this covers bases ... Romans & respectable Jewish elders. They handled his body; his dead body. It is clear when a body is dead. When the spirit has been handed over (even in animals) - It's such a weird feeling to be in the presence of a body that has no spirit, no life, but it is a very real sensation. And Nicodemus and Joseph of Arimathea felt that. They buried the body, they bound it with burial clothes and spices - which means they probably spent at least an hour with the dead body of Jesus, and quite likely 2-4 hrs. ... Meanwhile, what is the spirit of Jesus doing? Fascinating. What are the apostles/ disciples of Jesus doing? They were not the ones burying him? What were they DOing? Thus, these two men touch me - they touch my heart; they feel important, they feel worthy of acknowledgment, respect, admiration, blessings. ... They seem special, but all I know of them (so far) is these few things.

The nearing of death - wow! And then to be "crucified" on the preparation day for Passover. wow! And all of this happens in the spring. When new growth is happening, when we emerge from the darkness and cold of winter - especially in the higher latitudes of the Northern Hemisphere. For closer to the equator (Jerusalem?) I wonder if the emergence of Spring is as noticeable. It is certainly noticeable here, in Atlanta, in the Southern United States - the dogwoods, the redbuds all blooming now; how fascinating.

Other interesting contextual pieces to consider are the stretch of the Roman Empire; the rule of Caesar ("Augustus"), the role of the Jews, the Romans, and others at that time. How far did the Roman Empire stretch at that time? What was happening elsewhere? In Italy, for example? And was this more like the "Republic" than the "Empire" at this moment in History? What did Jesus know of his context? Being in his early 30's? Wow. And then in the first 100 years after Jesus' life - to think it was the greatest extent and "height" of the Roman Empire! All of France, all of Britain, all of the Iberian Peninsula, all of Greece and Macedonia and Turkey... Egypt.... all of the lands bordering the Mediterranean Sea. All of this, just after the life of Jesus! This has many implications - #1) the travelers of stories; the proliferation of the stories of his works. And there are others.

Today is Good Friday. Only once a year. This is the time when the pollen count is high. I feel it in my throat, my lungs, my eyes. These stories are awesome. They are incredible. Something was known by these "characters" over 2000+ years ago! They had access to a level of understanding that transcends the cacophony of "knowledge" of "wealth" - because these are treasures of Heaven - and they are here on Earth. How do we access them? through love, by truth, along the way of Light. If we live as children of light (light Nicodemus and Joseph) then the way will lead us to Treasures on Earth - those magical feelings of joy, connection, well-being, health, abundance, friendship ... it is all here now! We can heal ourselves. Lord God, please allow me to do so - to adore you with every breath, every movement, every thought, everything I DO. - to be of Heaven and a Blessing to the Earth - to live my life as Light. wow!

The Hebrews, the Greek, the Romans (Latin) - three languages; three pa-

triarchal cultures... and what of the women? what of the children? what of Nature? What of the sacred rhythms of the earth... and then the British (and the Celts) and now Americans (north and south). What have we learned from Jesus? What will I do with what I know? There is more to life than empires and knowledge and fame - there is this current life of humankind; and if we do not learn as a culture(s) and do as we've learned, then we may be forgotten from the Earth and the future of its inhabitants. Wow. Dear God, I adore you - let us be Blessed. Let us BE a Blessing and DO as Blessed - Lights unto this world.

Amen.